Journey to
the Well

First published in Ireland in 2021 by
HACHETTE BOOKS IRELAND

1

Cataloguing in Publication Data is available from the British Library

ISBN: 978 1 52938 233 4

Book design and typesetting: Anú Design, Tara
Printed and bound in Great Britain by Clays Ltd, Elcograf, S.p.A.

Hachette Books Ireland's policy is to use papers that are natural, renewable and
recyclable products and made from wood grown in sustainable forests.
The logging and manufacturing processes are expected to conform to the
environmental regulations of the country of origin.

Hachette Books Ireland
8 Castlecourt Centre
Castleknock
Dublin 15, Ireland

A division of Hachette UK Ltd
Carmelite House, 50 Victoria Embankment, EC4Y 0DZ

www.hachettebooksireland.ie

Journey to the Well

Connecting to Celtic Ways and Wisdom

MARY KENNEDY &
DEIRDRE NÍ CHINNÉIDE

HACHETTE
BOOKS
IRELAND

with gratitude to our celtic ancestors
for the gifts of resilience, courage
and the reminder of where we have
come from and who we can be ...

contents

introduction: journeying in

Water, the old stories tell us, flows up from sources in the Otherworld and gushes out into the rivers ...

– From *If Women Rose Rooted* by Sharon Blackie

Since long before the time of the early Christian church in Ireland, the well has been recognised as a place of healing. Held deep within the earth, a journey to the well nurtured and refreshed the pilgrim who drank of its healing waters.

For both of us sisters, from our earliest days, 'the well' has had significance, specifically St Brigid's well. We grew up on St Brigid's Road in Clondalkin, Dublin 22, and around the corner on Boot Road was a well named for the saint.

For so many Irish people, the lore around our female patron saint is familiar, and Brigid has a special place in our hearts. Our female patron saint was a woman of substance, spanning the pagan and the Christian worlds. She was born around AD 450 to a Christian mother and a father who was a pagan chieftain of Leinster. The lore goes that when she laid down her cloak on the land her father had promised her, it grew and spread to cover sufficient space for her monastery.

Growing up on St Brigid's Road was like living in an extended community, where everyone knew each other well. Our mam, Pauline, and her sister Eilish had a double wedding and bought houses side by side, so we lived very close to our cousins, sharing holidays, special events like Christmas and birthdays, as well as everyday life with them. All the neighbours were very close too and at times the road felt like an extended playground where, on summer days, we returned to the house only to be fed and watered.

The well around the corner – a regular meeting place with friends on summer evenings – was sadly often in a sorry state of neglect. But each year, in the run-up to St Brigid's Day, we were sent by the nuns to partake in a clean-up. Rubbish would be removed from the holy waters: everything from plastic bags to newspapers to shopping trolleys, the grass verges would be trimmed and all in all it would be restored to something more fit to honour a deity, even if we saw it less as act of devotion to St Brigid than some diversion from school. Brigid's Day itself was a day off school. Crosses were made from rushes that were gathered in a nearby field and we often took a trip down to the local well.

Thus, our journeys to the well began, perhaps less holy than practical, yet somehow unconsciously embedding within us some sense of renewal, of possibility, that springs from journeying to the well.

Happily, in recent times that well has been taken in hand and restored to its appropriate state. It is a place of prayer and intercession, highly regarded by local people and others who travel there and leave mementos as part of their devotion to Brigid.

There are many traditions associated with the saint: the Brigid's Cross and the *Brat Bhríde* (Brigid's cloak) to name but two. They remind us of an Irish woman with a loving, caring heart, a woman of strength, courage and determination. Her feast day on 1 February heralds the beginning of brighter days, of rebirth and growth, as we emerge from the darkness of the winter months and proceed with hope and light in our hearts.

Perhaps it is a fitting analogy for the position we find ourselves in at this time. There is no doubt that we are living through harrowing and challenging times. As we emerge from almost two years of uncertainty, we are faced with the task of planning and plotting our course, redefining our sense of Being, of Becoming, in a changed world.

Being at home through an enforced lockdown has brought both gifts and challenges to our doors. We are seeking rebirth and growth as we emerge from the darkness of the virus that took over our world and our lives. We want to have hope and light in our hearts, to find meaning and a sense of the spiritual in our redefined, everyday lives, to go on a journey of spiritual self-discovery.

We believe that our rich Celtic heritage and spirituality can give us the strength and the courage of Brigid and other major figures from our culture and Celtic past, to find comfort and optimism as we take our place in a different reality, setting out on uncharted waters.

In these pages, we draw on Deirdre's Aran Islands connection – her adopted home – a place where the link to Celtic spiritualty remains vibrant and alive. It is here that Deirdre composed *Celtic Passage*, a spiritual musical journey, and where she opened up her spiritual retreat centre on the island of Inis Mór, after years of work in the field of psychotherapy, among other things working with victims of war trauma in the Balkans.

As we cross a threshold following this deeply significant time, we hope that this book can be a companion, a place to stop and dip into its waters from time to time, and to find there something that will hold you in a spirit of friendship, with other *anam caras* or soul friends, along the way.

Sisters and brothers, we invite you to join us as we gather to heal and to seek guidance on our way. We draw from our own experiences and challenges over the years, sharing stories, insights and reflections, as we invite you to listen to your own voice, to look into your own inner well and find gifts and blessings of the heart's journey.

We have invited Brigid to be our guide through the Celtic seasons of *Samhain*, *Imbolg*, *Bealtaine* and *Lughnasa*, drawing on her qualities and gifts. She is the embodiment of the Divine Feminine in each of our seasons, appearing as the crone or wise woman in winter, the young bride of spring, the goddess of summer and the eternal mother of autumn. Each time we meet her she becomes a teacher and friend who guides us through the changing seasons of the Celtic calendar. As you drink from the inner well of life experience with the support of this powerful woman, we hope you find something there to nourish, refresh and renew you.

Let us cross this threshold together, so that as we re-emerge and move towards new lands, we feel held, guided and encouraged to trust the heart that leads us gently in hope.

At each new land,
There is a Cross.
A place to stop and scan direction.
It is here you will be tempted to remain
The same old story
Of a self that was,
Cornered by its frame.
Take my Hand, little One,
Let you walk on the inside,
Saved from that which blocks
Your journey Home,
To this Good House of Hope.

– 'New Lands' Deirdre Ní Chinnéide

samhain

The Celtic Season of Winter

introduction

*Stay a little longer, mooring in the harbour of your heart.
Anchored there forever.*

– From 'Forgotten', *Celtic Passage*

The Celtic year begins on 1 November at *Samhain*, a time
of stillness and darkness, when seeds that are planted rest
in the anticipation of the light that awaits above ground. In
the Celtic tradition, our ancestors lived in close connection
with the natural world. They followed the journey of the sun
as a guide through the seasons that surrounded them on a
daily basis. Crossing over into a new season was seen as a
move beyond a threshold, and was duly marked with rituals
that included blessings and incantations and involved the
whole community, who honoured the land upon which they

depended for survival. The water well was the source from which communities drew in all seasons, with its life-giving properties understood to manifest beyond the physical into the metaphysical, its spiritual properties central to the source of their spirituality. In our *Samhain* journey to the well, we will draw on ancient Celtic wisdom.

Inspired by the Celtic calendar, and observing its close connection to the natural rhythms of life, we will travel from the depths and darkness of winter to the rebirth of spring and the fullness of light. *Samhain* literally translates as 'summer's end', and marks the beginning of the Celtic New Year, the threshold of the depths and darkness of winter. The earth rests as the fullness of harvest gives way to stillness; the land waits for the return of the sun and the renewal that comes with spring. The threshold time of *Samhain* is regarded as a thin veil between everyday life and the spirit world, when the spirits of the dead are free to roam and the presences of loved ones who have died are nearby. Fires were traditionally lit to brighten the darkness and call in the ancestors and spirits of those who had passed on to the world of *Slí na Fírinne*, or 'way of truth'. Halloween or *Oíche Shamhna* is a clear example of how people dress up as witches and ghosts and take on the persona of a spirit from the other world. It is a healthy way of playing with quite a mysterious realm and on the Aran Islands, it continues to be celebrated by many members of the community.

Adults as well as children go to great lengths to pick a costume that totally disguises them. The night begins with people leaving their doors open as a welcome to the spirits who visit their home. In silence the spirits enter and sweets and treats are left on the kitchen table as a gift to the *pucaí* that come from far and wide. Local pubs are full of strange characters that night and their identity is kept strictly secret. Prizes are given to the most imaginative costumes and it is only at the end of the night that masks are taken off to reveal the people behind the weird and wonderful characters. It is said that it is a great night to have fun in the local bar (especially if you have been barred but can have free and easy access on this mischievous night).

At this time, *An Chailleach* – the witch or crone figure – dresses in the black cloth of winter and asserts herself as the wise voice of the earth and the darker season. By times she was feared and celebrated and her powerful presence dominates this time. What might her cloaked wisdom have to offer us? What might she want to impart to us about the resting time, the transformation that can happen when we give way to stillness, when we listen to our deepest inner voice, especially in the heart of darkness?

In 2019, when a new type of coronavirus arrived in the world, it brought in its wake a pandemic of illness and chaos, an unprecedented state of altered living, globally. In ancient times, a force such as this might have been understood as a deeply threatening spirit, heralding states of fear, loss and uncertainty. With the arrival of Covid-19, little did we know that we would be called into a prolonged *Samhain* time, one of darkness and a loss of a way of life that had kept our world turning in familiar, predictable ways.

We are living in strange and challenging times. Extended

periods of 'lockdown' have become part of our realities. It is a time of huge uncertainty, fear and 'dis-ease'. Where is this road leading us? Who has the roadmap? How do we navigate our way from this darkness into the light? Our hope here is to lean into this journey, taking time to reflect and draw water from our own inner well, and together creating a roadmap to a place of nourishment and renewal, with a shared vision of what we can learn and how we can integrate this time.

We invite you to join us in reflecting honestly on how we have negotiated this unexpected, extended *Samhain*. We share our own stories in the hope they will encourage you to engage with yours. Drawing from the voices of our ancestors, together we can cross a threshold of exploration and possibility, where our spirits are renewed. Fionn Mac Cumahail, a great hero of mythology, spoke of listening and being restored to the present moment and by being present to the reality of our times, to hear 'music of what happens'. Celebrating new notes, we can connect to the song that offers us hope, singing us home to a new and changed reality.

mary

Help me to find my happiness in my acceptance of what is my purpose. In friendly eyes, in work well done. In quietness born of trust and most of all in the awareness of spirit in my being.

This ancient Celtic prayer has always had a resonance for me. It sums up very clearly the qualities that undoubtedly lead to a calm and gentle acceptance of what's important in life. There's great self-awareness in a desire to have purpose, friendship, diligence, trust and a spiritual dimension to our lives. Wouldn't it be lovely if we could harness those positive and meaningful qualities and use them to guide us through this uncharted landscape, this changed reality?

Personally, navigating life through Covid-19 was an emotional rollercoaster, careering through fear, acceptance, anger, sadness, lethargy, guilt, serenity and contentment. Quite the gamut of emotions – and wait for it: they hit me in … no particular order! That gamut was reminiscent of the ways that *Samhain* can throw many harsh weather patterns at us. Covid was very definitely my winter storm!

Everyone will agree, I think, that there was a sameness to life from the beginning of the pandemic. Why then did I wake up feeling energised and motivated one day and yet the following morning, it was hard to summon the enthusiasm to get out of bed?

Back in March 2020, I was quite sanguine as the beginnings of change started to be felt. I had retired from presenting RTÉ's *Nationwide* at the end of 2019 and had been excited to embark on the new adventure that took me far outside my comfort zone, being part of *Dancing with the Stars*. I'm looking forward to telling you all about that wonderful experience in another chapter. For now, suffice it to say it was a seven-day-a-week commitment and the plan was to follow the dancing with some time relaxing and travelling during spring and summer, visiting new places, catching up with friends that my filming schedule with *Nationwide* had meant I'd seen too rarely. You know, though, what they say: 'Man proposes and God disposes!'

Within two weeks of finishing on *Dancing with the Stars*, Ireland went into lockdown. At first, I was glad of the opportunity to slow down, take stock and simply live in the moment. I enjoyed the gentler pace of life, the time in the garden, the decluttering. I was content right through that period with one fairly notable exception. My first grandchild, Patrick Sonny Boland, turned one in April that year and I hated the fact that I couldn't travel to Limerick to blow out the candle with him and his mam and dad. My daughter Eva and her husband, Benny, moved into their newly renovated house in Limerick city just as the first lockdown came into force. It was good timing for them, but I won't lie, it was a little heart-breaking for Paddy's nana because, while the restoration work was being carried out, they'd lived with me in Dublin.

I went from seeing Paddy every day to not seeing him at all, and sadness took over for a while as his first birthday passed without me being able to be with him. That was followed closely by guilt, being so aware of those who were suffering huge loss in those early days of the virus. Who was I to feel sorry for myself when there were people unable to visit their loved ones in residential homes? People were dying alone in hospitals and homes, without seeing their loved ones in their final hours. By comparison, I knew I had nothing to be sad about. And yet I was sad. I realised, of course, that a first birthday goes over the head of the main celebrant, and in fairness to Eva and Benny, they did organise a little party for Paddy. He sat at the top of the table in his party hat, surrounded by four teddies, also wearing party hats and enjoying individual bowls of jelly and ice cream! (Who actually ate the four desserts has never been disclosed.)

My memory of the first lockdown is, for the most part, quite positive. It was a time to reboot, to reflect on the important things in life. The sun shone, the birds sang, the incidence of infection, suffering and death fell and everybody breathed a sigh of relief. I appreciated the simple things of life in a renewed and refreshed way.

Many of us would probably agree that we took much for granted before this pandemic invaded our world and turned our lives upside down. We were used to having freedom to travel, to meet friends for a drink or a meal, to be surrounded by loved ones for special occasions. All of that was a thing of the past when the pandemic struck and we were confined and frightened. Thankfully, when the restrictions of lockdown ended, the wonder returned, and I took nothing for granted. I was grateful for the opportunity to see my close friends and family again. I remember the joy of being allowed to travel outside my county. I was delighted that staycations were the order of the day and that people who would previously have holidayed abroad were exploring and enjoying our beautiful country. The *Nationwide* message was definitely getting through!

I have to admit that, when restrictions were reintroduced in December 2020, my resilience became increasingly depleted and I found that Christmas particularly hard. People who know me understand that family, friends, colleagues and neighbours are what make my life meaningful and joyous. Sixteen people gathered around the Christmas table in 2019. A year later, there were five. It was a lonely, dark time. I felt sadness and, once again, guilt because there were so many people worse off than me. The long, dark days of *Samhain* rested heavily on my shoulders and threw shadows across my psyche. The New Year didn't herald much change. New strains of the virus invaded our shores. The lockdown continued. I found it harder to self-motivate, to maintain structure in my day. Some days, just getting out of bed was hard. I missed people, occasions, gatherings. Like many others, I was frustrated at times, angry at the slow pace of the vaccination rollout, the continued arrivals to our airports and ports. I was irritable, below par. My emotional well was dry and I struggled through these dark days, forcing myself to go for a jog. Invariably, I felt better for the physical activity, but the emotional baseline for 'better' was fairly low to begin with. I did take consolation from the fact that we were doing the right thing and that lockdown was saving lives. There was a feeling of solidarity with people in other countries who were suffering also.

That Celtic prayer took on a new relevance with its references to acceptance, trust, quietness and even friendly eyes – all that was visible behind masks. The spirit of my Celtic self was being tested for sure, that spirit of connection to others, to the earth and to community that was placed to one side for good reason.

The moments of acceptance brought with them the grace of a realisation that 'this too shall pass'. I acknowledged my sadness, my loneliness, my guilt and I allowed myself to find the pandemic and its restrictions difficult and horrible. I slowly arrived at a point of understanding that I was mourning the good parts of life pre-Covid, and that it was okay to do so. This realisation helped me to cope with the loss of social contact and the fear that this ongoing pandemic was taking valuable time from my life.

At sixty-seven years of age, I'm well aware I have less time ahead of me than I have already lived. That fear of time lost was corrosive and was inhibiting my enjoyment of the present moment. I accepted this after a while and, as a result, the fear lessened. Just as *Samhain* takes us on a journey through darkness and gradually brings us into the light of a new season, my emotions evolved during the different stages of the pandemic. They travelled through some periods of darkness before reaching a place of peace, of understanding of this unprecedented period in our lives, a time that has shaped me as I proceed towards the next chapter of my life.

I realise that I am not unique in the way I have travelled on that rollercoaster since March 2020, and I hope that what I have described resonates with readers. It's always nice to feel that we're not alone in a challenging situation.

One of the consolations of this troubled period has been the sense that this is a shared journey. We Irish are lucky, I believe, to have a rich Celtic heritage and history that informs the way we think, we feel, we live our lives. *Is ar scáth a chéile a mhairimid*. We live in the shadow of each other. As a tribe, we connect easily with others. We are resilient. We work hard and we play hard. We are reflective, caring people with a spiritual dimension to our lives. All of this gives meaning to our acceptance of Covid restrictions to keep ourselves and others safe and to our joy at the easing of those restrictions which facilitated that interaction once again. Deirdre and I hope that by exploring personal experiences and dipping into our shared Celtic well, we will achieve solace and consolation and a vision of hope for our future in an adjusted world.

deirdre

Living on the Aran Islands, a wild and isolated place located off the western coast of Ireland – next stop America – can seem, to people visiting the island for the first time, like a strange choice. The rhythm and pace of life is different here and the state of lockdown – or forced isolation – is not anything new and is felt at various times, such as when severe weather prevents us reaching the mainland.

When I first came to the island in around 1988, I saw it as a chance to take time out from the busyness and activity of city life, the fulfilment of an inner desire to slow down, to be still in a quiet, peaceful place. Working as a therapist in the Dublin Rape Crisis Centre brought with it challenging experiences, and heading to the island gave me a great opportunity to rest in a very different reality and landscape. When real lockdown hit, though, it was, of course, no one's choice, and we all had to adapt in unforeseen ways.

Mary describes well the emotions that I, too, journeyed with – from fear, initially, to sadness and loneliness, to surrendering to what is a changed reality, trying to see and experience it in new and more creative ways.

The Aran Islands are steeped in Celtic history and heritage. Habitation of Inis Mór dates back to pre-Christian times and for a small place – 13 km long and 3 km wide – it has an incredible number of ruins and sacred sites that hold great mystery in who they housed over the generations. You can wander to a holy well, a ruined church, a beehive hut or visit one of the many spectacular forts including Dún Aonghasa and the Black Fort, which, to my mind, are some of the greatest wonders of the world. Taking time to rest and listen in one of these amazing forts leads you to wonder about the community that lived here in the past and the legacy that they still seem to watch over in the power and presence of this inspiring landscape.

Over recent months, I've had time to reflect and to consider the lineage and heritage of our ancestors, who survived adverse and difficult times in their lives. Being cut off from the mainland brings a challenge and there is a sense that the people who chose to live in these extreme places had a good reason for doing so. Their homes were often strategically located near a well and their interest and reverence for the natural journey of the sun and moon meant that their sacred sites were built to align with the solstice and equinox times of the year. Being self-sufficient was vital and being so close to nature and the raging seas, they experienced both inner and outer storms that inevitably brought them through new and uncharted waters.

On the island, the ancestral tradition of walking to the well was a quest for physical and spiritual nourishment and healing, especially during challenging times. Seven stones were held as pilgrims walked around the well, in the direction of the sun, quietly praying their intention in the silence of their own hearts.

Inis Mór is known as the island of saints and scholars because of all the saints who came and spent time here, studying and living a contemplative and monastic life. Saints Ciaran, Enda, Asurnai, Colmcille, to name but a few, are honoured and remembered as people walk to the well on the celebration of their feast days.

The area around the well is tidied and flowers and candles adorn the route as pilgrims make their journey in prayer and intercession to the guidance and protection of those saints and scholars who lived here long ago. The well to St Colmcille rests on the eastern shore of the island and on his feast day, it is magical to step over the rocky shore, quietly walk the rounds of the well and sit gazing towards the mainland on the horizon, which must have seemed like heaven on earth to the people who gathered here long ago.

No words are spoken and the silence brings a reverent presence to the community, respecting the petitions held firmly in the heart and offering the pilgrims a deep connection to the spirit of those who lived and prayed here from generation to generation. It was W.B. Yeats who told J.M. Synge to go and live with the people of the islands to know them and the preciousness of their culture and heritage that is deeply rooted in the Celtic Soul.

How wonderful it is to see how that journey of the heart can still inform us in the search for a connectedness, giving a deep meaning to our lives today. There is a sense that we have forgotten this connection, but perhaps it is time to remember, especially if we take time to listen to the stirrings and the wisdom of our own heart's journey.

As we journey deeper into the mystery of *Samhain* and what it might offer us, we give thanks to all that sustains us as we drink from the well.

With gratitude for the inner strength that has helped us navigate challenging times, let us listen to our hopes and intentions as we journey deeper into a reflection of *Samhain*.

lost in lockdown

deirdre

At 5.00pm each day the last boat leaves the island of Inis Mór and all who sail in her head back towards the shores of the mainland, to Rossaveel, Connemara. Whoever is on the island is locked in, so to speak, till the ferry returns the following morning. I love this time when the last boat departs and it almost feels as if the island breathes a sigh of relief at a job well done, welcoming, feeding, entertaining and showing its beauty to people from all over the world. It is as if a quiet silence returns following the business of the day, where up to a thousand tourists arrive here in the height of the summer season.

Imagine the change in atmosphere, as the island closed its shores to visitors in an effort to keep coronavirus far from this small offshore community. Tensions flared between those who wanted to keep businesses open and those who were willing to let the tourist season go for a year, concentrating on keeping the islands and its people safe and well. Almost overnight, schools, pubs, restaurants and shops — except for our local Spar – closed and remained closed. I remember on one particular day, seeing the boat leave with just two passengers, the nurse and guard changing shifts and returning home to their families on the mainland.

All changed, changed utterly and yet, in many ways, the island always lends itself to a form of lockdown by offering an isolated experience and a different way of life. A local fisherman mending his nets on a warm sunny day said that he felt the island had returned to how it was twenty years ago and welcomed the fact that people had more time for each other, connecting in a way that brought them into socially distanced chats while out walking the meandering paths through the fourteen small villages dotted on the landscape of Inis Mór.

The clusters of houses in these small villages are almost mirror images of the different dwellings that the island has been home to over generations. The ancient forts, holy wells and ruined churches, some of which date back to the third and fourth centuries, became the homes and places of worship for spiritual communities that lived and listened in this landscape over time.

In the early Christian church, the island was home to different groups of monks, who were often sent to places of great extremity to live and pray in beehive huts, spending long periods in isolation.

With no distractions, the idea was to be open to God's meaning in all that they experienced. Their lockdown was a chosen one and yet the purpose was to live the monastic life with a close connection to the land and the presence and guidance of God in all seasons and stirrings of the heart and soul. Perhaps in time, like these monks, we can reflect on our lockdown experience to see if and how it has changed us in new and unexpected ways.

Lockdown, for me, was a journey through both calm and stormy waters that brought days of total desolation, surrender and a need to find creative ways to negotiate this strange and challenging time.

Arriving back in Ireland following a concert and retreat I facilitated in California, it wasn't long before all my work had been cancelled and, like so many, I was faced with the uncertainty of how I would continue to pay bills and the mortgage and keep some kind of hope in a situation where everything just seemed to be falling apart. That initial stage of not knowing what was happening and where it would all lead was terrifying. I was relying totally on the daily news about the global development of a crisis that was bringing the world to a virtual standstill.

While struggling with extreme isolation and loneliness at times, there was also a feeling of gratitude to be in a safe and beautiful place and to watch and listen to how the world was managing from afar. Often the islanders say that they are going back to *Ireland* when they take a trip to the mainland, and being here 'on the rock', as it is fondly described, can feel like being in an in-between place, where the veil is thin between this world and other worlds of a spiritual nature. *Samhain* is one of those times considered to be a portal when the spirits are especially welcome and considered quite near. My good friend and neighbour would regularly light candles in her garden at night in memory of those who had passed on to the other world, *Slí na Fírinne*.

The local priest and church services have always been of utmost importance to the local people and having to shift all of these services online brought with it great confusion and frustration for many, especially the older islanders with very little interest or skill in computers and technology. There is an abundance of the most beautiful sacred places dotted around the landscape and people were regularly seen visiting these sites, in the absence of being able to gather in their local church.

We were so blessed in the lovely weather to walk, swim, cycle and enjoy the carpet of wildflowers that is particular to the landscape of Inis Mór. In his poem '*Na Blátha Craige*', Liam Ó Flaithearta, an island poet, addresses the flowers and asks them how they survive in such a harsh and rocky landscape.

'*Táimid faoi dhraíocht ag ceol na farraige*,' they reply. We are under the magic of the music of the sea.

It is that music that continues to soothe and bless the time I spend on the island and it is also the sound that touches the hearts of many visitors who step onto the island of saints and scholars. These islands hold a tradition and spirituality that can, I think, inform and guide us gracefully through recent stormy waters. The silence and a sense of timelessness here encourage an attention to the colours of the changing seasons, the birdsong echoing from dawn to dusk and the breeze that sings through stone.

The light heart lives long.

– Irish proverb

mary

By lockdown three, a dark night of the soul for so many of us, the process of writing this book became a saving grace, as I travelled into our Celtic past and engaged with our rich heritage.

We are a resilient race. We have struggled and survived through the ages, from the time our ancestors were consumed by the need to clear forests for habitation and farming, through wars with the Danes, Normans and English, through famine times, uprisings, a war of independence and a civil war. We emerged from all of those trials without losing our positive, can-do attitude to life, or our connection with people around us.

The age-old tradition of the *meitheal oibre* endures to this day, where farmers help each other out with haymaking and other time-dependent tasks at different moments in the agricultural calendar. It's not just in farming circles that you will encounter the *meitheal* in operation. When Deirdre moved into her home on Inis Mór, the whole family, along with some friends, travelled to the island and got out the ladders, the paint and paint brushes and, over a long weekend, gave what was formerly a restaurant a lovely makeover. We were fed well and the sun shone during this time of hard work, warm hospitality and lots of laughs.

We are also a nation of storytellers. The old tradition of *bothántaíocht*, whereby people would go to neighbours' houses in the evening, tell stories and sing songs, is not an everyday occurrence anymore as it was in the days of Peig Sayers on the Great Blasket Island, and in other rural communities across the land, but we Irish still love a good gathering and sing-song.

A tradition that endures strongly in parts of Ireland is the *Pátrún*, or Stations, the annual house mass hosted by a different family every year, demonstrating a nice mix of community, spirituality and hospitality. Again, in the *meitheal* spirit, neighbours put their shoulder to the wheel, making preparations and providing plenty of food, extra crockery, and whatever else the host family needs for this special day.

The *Pátrún* may not extend throughout the whole country these days but compassion and warmth do. Every sports club in Ireland depends on volunteers, willing to coach a team, wash the gear, cut the grass. Volunteerism is part of what we are as a people. We saw many lovely examples of people reaching out to others during the lockdowns. For me, focusing on these characteristics, our resilience, our sense of community, of compassion and our spirituality gave me consolation during the dark days of lockdown three. When I was feeling very low and lacking motivation, I reminded myself of the combination of strength and gentleness that we have gained from our Celtic ancestry and that gave me comfort.

It is salutary to remember those frustrating and difficult days, and the struggle to retain a sense of wellbeing as they pushed on, seemingly interminably.

With the darkness comes frustration: what toll is this ongoing state of affairs having on our national mental health? The news media is full of stories of people feeling that they cannot take much more of these really severe restrictions. There is anger and jostling for position. Depending on your point of view, there are too many restrictions, or not enough. Hotel quarantine can't come fast enough, or is a waste of time. It can be hard to know what to think.

My daily routine involves going for a 5 km run. It's within the guidelines, 2.5 km out and the same on the way back. There's an uneasy feeling with those I pass that we are all watching each other, slightly warily. I don't blame people who are sticking to the letter of the law being annoyed with others who are a bit lax in their lockdown habits. But there's a need for a bit of understanding and flexibility here. I try to ground myself in the fact that we never know what is going on in people's lives, their struggles, mental, physical, emotional.

I always feel the better for my daily run yet sometimes I just can't be bothered. A cycle of self-pity, guilt and anger can run its course instead. One week I sit at home and feel sorry for myself, then the next week I berate myself thinking about those who are locked down in truly difficult circumstances. And on it goes. I know this isn't my best self, but *Samhain* has me in its grip and I struggle to release myself.

I have never been a good sleeper, but the land of nod has all but eluded me in recent weeks. I have resigned myself to the fact that my sleeping pattern is chaotic. I go to bed early, read a good book and gratefully nod off. I put the book away and turn off the light. Bad move! All of a sudden, I am wide awake. I listen to a sleep-inducing meditation, to no avail, so I read again until silly o'clock and then fall asleep, glasses on, book in hand. There are nightmares. One night, Apaches on horseback are chasing me through snow. I look forward to getting that one interpreted some day!

Anxiety dogs me. My normally calm, fairly unflappable self seems to have deserted me. A job, virtually hosting a business gathering, which wouldn't have cost me a thought before, now causes me to go over and over my notes until it is time for the event. So much uncertainty, restriction, self-doubt.

I'm conscious that there are upcoming family occasions that should be joyous but won't be celebrated together in person again this year – my grandson's second birthday, my daughter Lucy's thirtieth, Deirdre's sixtieth. The self-catering cottage I booked for the end of May starts to look iffy. But I have a lot to be thankful for. My family is healthy. I have a garden. I am active.

We are constantly being told that we are 'all in this together', but that doesn't make it the same for everyone. I know there are others living in much sadder and more difficult circumstances.

If *Samhain* brings the darkest night, it also signals that we have *Imbolg* to look forward to, with its promise of light. Contemplation, forbearance and an enduring sense of community are traits embodied in Brigid, whose feast day heralds the beginning of spring with its lengthening days and brighter skies. Brigid was a strong woman, resilient, compassionate, outgoing and spiritual. She will guide us from the darkness into the light of *Imbolg*. This prayer from the diocese of Kildare and Leighlin, Brigid's spiritual home, speaks to that desire for light and strength within us all.

Shine your light where there is darkness,
strengthen me in any weakness.
Heal all within that may be ill.

Love and Loss

deirdre

The Celtic world is known for a particular honouring of the *Art of Living*, reflecting on one's life, meaning and purpose, and the *Art of Dying*, where death is seen not as an end but as an opening to another state of awareness and a return home to an eternal place of rest.

> *There is a time for everything, and a season*
> *for every activity under the heavens ...*
> *a time to be born and a time to die.*
> *A time to plant and a time to uproot ...*
>
> *– Ecclesiastes 3*

It is a bright yet brisk morning, the mainland of Connemara glistening from across the deep blue sea that separates Inis Mór from the rest of Ireland. A group of us islanders stand together outside the house of Kate and John Dirrane, or John Bhaba Pheige as he is locally known, on the morning of 18 February, waiting for the door to open and the coffin, holding John's remains, to be carried by his son and grandsons and placed on the back of an open truck. Slowly and reverently, the truck will make its way to the local church followed by islanders, walking socially distant from each other and wearing masks in what seems like an intrusion on the faces of these people. We are gathering in grief, to say goodbye to a well-loved neighbour and friend. John was a gentle man, one of the oldest members of the community, and was married for well over sixty years. He had great stories from the past and was still cycling his bicycle up to recent years, as well as being noted as a fine dancer of an old-time waltz in the arms of his lifetime companion and darling wife, Kate.

It is often said that we Irish do death well ... a strange comment, but one to be proud of, in finding a healthy ritual and a way of marking and celebrating the life of someone as they cross a threshold that awaits us all at some stage in our future. The traditional wake, which is still alive and well on the islands, gives an opportunity to gather and share stories, to laugh, cry and remember the life of a person, while also supporting each other as a community through a shared experience of grief, love and loss.

Ritual is so important to help us grieve well and I remember the poignancy of being present at my first island funeral, standing by the pier, awaiting the arrival of the ferry carrying the coffin with the deceased person, making his last journey home. The silent presence of the community was palpable – people standing sentry-like, as a symbol of their welcoming and blessing of this soul on its arrival for a final ritual and a place of rest.

Islanders often continue that walk of silence behind the open truck as it makes its way to the home of the deceased, and the following day and night, people will come to visit the home and pay their respects to the grieving family. Prayers, including the rosary, are said at the end of the night and the sound of the Irish language, carried in the breeze as it is prayed by those who gather in the garden of the house to say one last goodbye to their neighbour and friend, is graceful and sacred. The body is never left alone on the night of the wake and some neighbours will offer to sit with the deceased while the family tries to rest before the funeral mass and burial the following day.

At the end of the funeral service, which takes place at the local church, the final journey and burial in the graveyard is again quite beautiful, where there is *sean nós* or old-style singing and traditional music is often played. Prayers are offered by the community, alongside the tradition of shovelling clay down on the coffin as it is placed in the open grave. This marks a real sense of returning to earth a loved one, who will be cradled in memory and in the soil of this mystical and ancient land.

We need to find ways to gather and to grieve, releasing tears that, in their shedding, bring us comfort, relief and a sense of support from all who come together at a difficult time. One of the most tragic aspects of dealing with death and loss during Covid has been the restriction of numbers at funerals, with families forced to decide who can attend a service and who has to watch the event online. Heart-breaking stories filled our television screens, of people not being able to visit their dying loved ones, or to hold the hand of their family member as they took their final breath, often dying alone or with the care, kindness and presence of already overstretched frontline workers. Being unable to gather and to grieve has had a traumatic effect on those who have been bereaved. So often we were reminded by a grieving daughter or son, who put pen to paper, that their mother or grandmother was not just a statistic to be included in the figures broadcast on the daily news. These were people who had stories and memories, hobbies and hopes that were taken away tragically as they lost their fight and life to Covid-19.

Our hearts will need to find ways to release this grief in time and to let go of the pain that many families have experienced as a result of this virus sweeping through our world. Laying wreaths in the Garden of Remembrance can of course help, but there will be a need to find ritual to ease the suffering felt by many as a result of huge loss and the inability to find comfort in a shared ritual and honouring of a life and love lost.

Samhain, beginning on 1 November in the Celtic Christian tradition, brings us across a threshold from All Saints, into All Souls' Day to a month dedicated in memory of those who have died. During November, on Inis Oírr, the smallest of the

Aran Islands, the children visit the graveyard on their way home from school and sit to light a candle or have a chat with their *maimeo* (grandmother) or *daideo* (grandfather), telling them the news from home or school in a very natural and innocent way.

Each year, on the island of Inis Mór, *searmanas Na Marbh* is held, a special ceremony remembering those who have gone from our sight but hold a special place in the well of our hearts ('*imithe as ár namharc, ach fós inár gcroíthe*'). The local church fills with people of all faiths and none, who gather together and, through silence, prayer, poetry, movement and music, honour the memory of those who have lost their lives during the year. A candle is brought to the altar as a symbol of each person who died and tears flow freely as the names are called and remembered with great fondness and affection. The church is decorated beautifully and there is a unique atmosphere, which brings people from far and wide for a healing ceremony, honouring and grieving the dead. Many say that it is one of the most important and significant rituals during the year, where they can stand together and collectively grieve and provide a prayer and space for much-needed healing of broken hearts, coping with the loss of loved ones. Great faith supports many people, believing in the nearness of the spirits of those who have died, often calling upon this 'communion of saints' to guide and support the daily challenges of everyday life. It is a healthy relationship and conversation with *death as an integral part of life*, and comes from living close to nature and the constant death and rebirth that the seasons bring to our door and shore.

As we transition as a society to face the challenges that lockdowns have brought, we can allow ourselves to open the heart and to feel those unshed tears that need to be welcomed as a normal response to a very abnormal experience worldwide. We are not alone and together we can learn to remember and to recall the heart, which is filled with love and memories for those who have died and who have struggled in any way, crossing this *Samhain* threshold from darkness into light.

Let us pause at the well to remember ...

In the rising of the sun and its setting,
We Will Remember Them.
In the blowing of the wind and in the chill of winter,
We Will Remember Them.
In the opening of the buds and in the rebirth of spring,
We Will Remember Them.
In the blueness of the sky and in the warmth of summer,
We Will Remember Them.
In the rustling of the leaves and in the beauty of autumn,
We Will Remember Them.
In the beginning of the year and when it ends,
We Will Remember Them.
When we are weary and in need of strength,
We Will Remember Them.
When we are lost and sick of heart,
We Will Remember Them.
When we have joys we yearn to share,
We Will Remember Them.
So long as we live,

They too shall live and
We Will Remember Them.

– Original translation of an old Irish litany of
prayer called 'Na Liodáin'

Let your life be a prayer,
Every movement ...
An invitation
To bless and caress.
Kneel softly
As you cradle stories,
Memories unravelling,
Seeds of sacred scripture.
Tears can moisten
Landscapes of the heart ...
And Holy is their name.

– Deirdre Ní Chinnéide

resilience

Ní neart go cur le chéile
There is no strength till we come together

– Old Irish saying

deirdre

My first experience with a Zoom call was a disaster. I had never heard of Zoom, but friends swore that this mode of technology could allow you to link in with all kinds of courses and programmes online, which would help relieve the challenge of suddenly finding myself with long days and weeks alone during the pandemic. Meditation has always been a great resource and I decided to get up early one morning, linking in with a Zoom class to see how I could connect with others for some virtual relaxation and community. On arrival, the facilitator was giving a talk, so I decided to shuffle about in my Christmas pyjamas, make breakfast and join in with the group on a well-nourished stomach. My microwave pinged on the cooking of porridge and I sang to my heart's content, knowing I would be heading into a very focused silence soon. Much to my horror, I was on camera, in full view, pottering around my kitchen, eventually named and shamed, muted and kicked out of my very first Zoom!

Following a period of mortification, it served me well to learn the details of how Zoom worked and it became one of the most important devices to bring the world into my home on the Aran Islands. As a family, we could now see each other online, feeling a little less alone and more resilient in an ever-changing world with restrictions that kept us at home and apart. It felt so important to connect with your tribe, so to speak, and to feel we could stay in touch and keep up with the family news.

'*Cé leis tú?*' is a question that is often asked here in this community. Its literal translation is 'Who owns you?', but what is really being asked is who are your people, your family, and where do you come from?

It must seem strange to some islanders when people from the mainland choose to come and live here permanently, especially when their family of origin is living somewhere else. Is there a dark secret as to why these 'blow-ins' land into the community that has lived together for generations? It was a big day for me when a local woman described me as '*Deirdre s'againne*' (our Deirdre) and I knew I had finally arrived.

My very first visit to the island was with Mary and our mam, Pauline. We arrived on a very wet and miserable day. I knew, though, that I would come back to this unique place and eventually settle here. Following the death of our mam in 2001, I ended up buying a house that had formerly been a restaurant we had visited together, and it was very special when Mary produced photos of us all that had been taken next to the fireplace. It felt that the spirit of Mam blessed and approved of this move to the island and it's lovely to have a picture of her by the fireplace, which is often known as *crói an tí*, or 'the heart of the home'.

Community has always been important for me and Inis Mór became a spiritual home, where that sense of belonging to the Celtic world nourished a shared love of language, culture and heritage. Growing up in Clondalkin was also wonderful and it was a privilege to be principal of Gaelscoil Chluain Dolcáin, an all-Irish primary school, and a member of Áras Chronáin Cultural Centre, both places with a great respect for language, culture and tradition. Being part of these groups brought a sense of belonging, an extended family of like-minded people and great opportunities to live and learn from the passion and resilience of others who had encountered many obstacles and challenges to hold on to something that they strongly believed in. I am always moved by the strength of the human spirit and have witnessed how supporting each other can help us all in the most challenging of situations.

'No man is an island' wrote John Donne and there is no doubt that we are stronger together than alone. The Celtic communities on the island built their forts in circular form, creating enclosed spaces where their people could be housed and embraced in a safe and nourishing environment.

There is an innate resilience in a people who live on a limestone rock in the Atlantic Ocean, weathering both internal and external storms. With a huge reliance on land and sea, there are many stories of families who lost loved ones through drowning or fishing tragedies.

Emigration also brought great sadness and loss to many families in days gone by and there was a tradition of gathering in a household for a wake before a loved one's departure. It is said that the ashes from the hearth were taken by the neighbours back to their house and would be returned on the celebration of the emigrant's return. Gleann na nDeor ('Valley of Tears') was a place on the island where people gathered to get a last look at the steamship passing as their loved one sailed off to foreign shores, in search of a new life and a stability that was hard to find at home.

Many of the poems and the songs in the *sean nós* or old-style tradition recount the heartache of their loss and offered a way for people to capture the pain of this experience, while creating great beauty and healing for others, in the sharing and singing of story and song. This longing for connection and drawing creatively on our well of resources to get us through adverse experiences is in many ways deep in our DNA. It has been clearly alive and well in the challenge of recent times.

Mary has a wonderful recall for memories and stories

from our family history, capturing the strength and resilience that our parents and grandparents passed on from generation to generation. They were not perfect by any means, but there is no doubt that for all of us who have managed to get through the extreme restrictions of recent times, there is and must be, as the song says, 'something inside so strong'.

mary

Our grandmother Annie Dowdall, who lived to the great age of 102, was a very resilient woman. Granny moved from Carlow to Dublin when she married in 1911 and she reared seven children in very turbulent times. When her first baby was due, she 'engaged a midwife', as she called it. The process involved standing on a chair in her back garden and calling to the woman whose house backed onto hers. Why? Because Granny had noticed the voluminous white aprons midwives wear hanging on the woman's clothesline and she knew she couldn't afford to have her baby in a nursing home.

She recounted stories of listening to Big Jim Larkin during the Great Lockout of 1913 and spoke of hiding her brothers' pistols under the mattress in the pram at the time of the Easter Rising. She managed to keep her family well during the Spanish flu epidemic in 1918 but lost Billy, one of her two sons, to tuberculosis, at the age of twenty-three. Shortly afterwards, her husband, Kit, a labourer in Guinness, died, leaving her with six children just before the outbreak of the

Second World War. Ration books and food coupons were the order of the day then, but the family survived and thrived and came out the other side.

Of Granny's family of seven children, our mother, Pauline, was the third and the apple didn't fall far from the tree. Mam left school at fifteen and got a job that she was obliged to leave when she got married. There was never much money to spare but she was a resourceful and resilient woman – and also self-sacrificing: her portions were always the smallest at mealtimes. There's only so far you can stretch a pot of scrambled eggs. For her, education was key and she was determined that her children would have the opportunities that had eluded her. She knitted Aran cardigans to bring in an extra bit of money and took Irish classes at night so that she could help us with our Irish homework. Maybe unconsciously she knew that Deirdre would end up in a Gaeltacht community in the West of Ireland, where the jumpers she was knitting originated. She passed on a love of Irish to us all, but knitting is a skill that may have bypassed our generation!

> *I've had a great life Daniel, a long life. It hasn't always been easy, but you have to take the bad with the good.*

My heart melts when I think back to this letter, written during the first lockdown by Margaret Lynch, a centenarian, to her newborn great-grandson, Daniel, born exactly one hundred years and one day after her. Margaret had to make do with waving to Daniel and his family through her window when she was cocooning during the early stages of the coronavirus pandemic. Her letter was part of RTÉ's *Letters from Lockdown* and with every syllable, you can feel the warmth, the acceptance, the resilience. This is a woman who was born during the War of Independence, who had to collect food coupons for her wedding breakfast in 1945. A woman who raised six children and who volunteered for more than half her life with the Sisters of Charity. Her grandchildren and great-grandchildren called her Granny Chocolate Bun. No marks, therefore, for guessing what treats she provided when they visited her at her home. It would be understandable if Margaret was saddened or even depressed at being apart from her loved ones as she turned one hundred, at not being able to hold her thirty-first great-grandchild when he was born. Anything but! She remained positive throughout the lockdown and cocooning, and she got to cuddle Daniel during the summer, when the restrictions were lifted. Margaret died in November 2020. She showed strength of character to the end.

Three strong women – Granny, Mam, Margaret – generations apart, all of whom had an innate positive attitude that afforded them resilience and stood them in good stead in hard times. It is this attitude that is needed now as we grapple with the challenges of this modern-day pandemic.

I am in awe of the commitment, compassion and sheer endurance of healthcare workers who, on countless occasions, have gone above and beyond the call of duty to minister to the people in their care. All they asked of us was to play our part by abiding by the lockdown guidelines in order to keep hospital admissions down.

It was hard to be apart from loved ones for such a protracted period. As a species, we reach out to others, we touch, we hug, we kiss, we talk. Not being able to do this required a new way of being, an adjustment, a resilience.

And we rose to the occasion. Gardaí and postal workers delivered groceries to people confined to their homes. I have fond memories of the times we stood outside and applauded the frontline workers, the candles we lit to remember people who died with Covid, the bingo sessions on balconies in apartment complexes. All served to raise the spirits of the local community and added to its resilience to weather this storm.

In the Celtic tradition, the symbol for strength is the Dara Knot, an intricate design of intertwining lines that have no beginning and no end and represent the root system of the mighty oak tree. That strength, interconnection and concern for others have been very much a part of our lives always. No matter where you travel in the world, you will find Irish people willing to lend a hand. Irish people are known for their empathy, their readiness to help others. It's a special quality that we often take for granted, but it's something of which we should be very proud. Think of the numbers of Irish who emigrated in search of a better life and found support and friendship from their own kind who had gone before them. I have travelled widely in the developing world and in every place that I have visited, there were Irish people devoting their lives to helping those who were less well off.

deirdre and mary

Our Celtic heritage embodies traits of strength, generosity and resilience. We prevail through the dark days of *Samhain*, through hardship, turmoil, sickness, death. Our interconnection allows us to dig deep, to look out for each other and to see things through. We journey to the well with renewed hope and look forward to lighter, brighter days as we move towards *Imbolg*.

Grace

In this hour of wakefulness
When all around are sleeping
When dark is darker still
And the sounds of the night
Creep up on you ...
May the soft clouds
Gather to embrace you
Drifting towards
The Grace of an Awakening
A Still Lake
In this your troubled heart.

– Deirdre Ní Chinnéide

imbolg

Crossing the Threshold into Spring

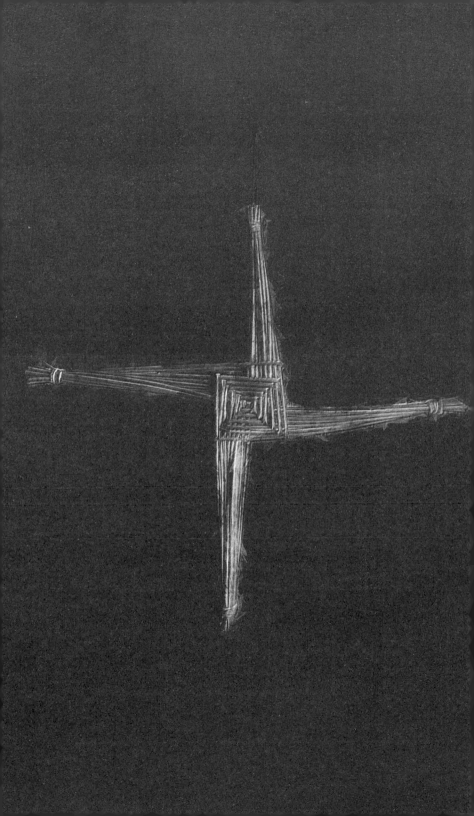

introduction

Anois teacht an earraigh,
Beidh an lá ag dul chun síneadh,
Is tar éis na Féile Bríde,
Árdóidh mé mo sheol.

Spring has come.
The days are getting longer
And after Brigid's Day,
I can hoist my sails again.

– 'Cill Aodáin' by Antaine Ó Raifteirí

deirdre

Imbolg is the name given to the threshold time celebrated on 1 February, St Brigid's feast day, and marks the slow awakening of the earth following the stillness and darkness of winter. Our *cailleach* or crone from *Samhain* changes shape into the young bride or *brídeog*, with the youthfulness of a young maiden as she invites us to cross the threshold towards the arrival of a season of growth and new life.

On Inis Meáin ('middle island'), the children make a *brídeog* or doll and visit the homes of their neighbours with a song and dance to bless the families and their livestock and crops for the year ahead.

> Bríd i mo chrios
> Muire 's a Mac
> Bríd 'Is a brat.
> Má 's fearr atá sibh anocht,
> Go mba seacht bhfearr a bheidh sibh
> Bliain ó anocht.

> *Brigid, Mary and her son, bless all here.*
> *May you be seven times better than you are now*
> *This time next year.*

– Traditional Irish prayer

It is so beautiful to see the children wander the boreens of the island carrying their *brídeog*, usually suspended on the arm of an old sweeping brush, and, of course, a little bag to gather money given to them by grateful recipients of their song and dance.

Who was this amazing woman honoured more and more each year in Ireland and other parts of the world? Brigid's charisma and message have travelled far and wide and there are schools and religious communities as far away as Australia that still honour her and the festival of *Imbolg*.

Peregrinatio means leaving one's homeland and wandering for the love of God in Latin. The early Christian monks are said to have stepped into a *currach* and let the breeze carry them wherever God wanted them to land. They trusted that by totally surrendering, they would eventually arrive at a new land and place of resurrection.

It is said that Brigid, who was born in Faughart, Co. Louth, around AD 450, found her place of resurrection in Kildare, where she built her monastery, cathedral and holy well. One intriguing aspect of her is that she is remembered as a goddess of the pre-Christian world and then brought into the church as abbess and saint. Her name means 'bridge'.

Each year on the eve of St Brigid's Day, I have the privilege of singing at a celebration of her life organised by the Brigidine sisters, who relit and have tended her flame at their centre, Solas Bhríde (Brigid's Light) in Kildare, since 1993. Hundreds of people from all over the world gather in the Japanese gardens, where rituals and stories are shared as an inspiration for our life and our world today. A Brigid's cross is woven around the fire and a candlelit pilgrimage is made by everyone to the holy well nearby. It is said that many healings are attributed to Brigid and a nearby tree is strewn with ribbons, rosary beads and symbols of gratitude for prayers and requests granted. This mystical woman dedicated her life to God and was known for her hospitality and welcome for all.

There is something magical each year in the powerful way she informs and inspires people from all over the world to open their inner journey, their deeper well. Everyone is given a piece of cloth to place outdoors that night, when it is said that Brigid touches the *Brat* or cloth with healing dew, which can bless and protect their families and loved ones during the year ahead.

Brigid was a prophet, a woman of the earth and a patron of poetry, smithcraft and healing. She also enjoyed an odd tipple or two and once described heaven as *a great lake of beer,* a great comfort, I am sure, for many a soul on their way to their eternal rest!

The Brigid's crosses, made from rushes, were placed over the doors to protect the hearth, home and animal stores on the eve of St Brigid's Day.

It is lovely to remember that sense of a female energy of power and protection, embracing and guarding all forms of new life. If developed in education, perhaps this could be a very real inspiration for young people in particular, connecting back to the wisdom of a woman who followed her dream and lived in love and harmony with herself, her community and the earth.

There is talk of making her feast day a national holiday as each year there is a rekindling of her story at places associated with her throughout the land. What an interesting balance of male and female we would have if Brigid, as well as Patrick, was celebrated as one of our patron saints.

Brigid is someone who is turning up more and more in my

life, not as a historical figure but as someone who embodies a presence and a passion for peace. Healing was an important part of who she was and, as a woman of peace, it is said that she made every effort in her work and ministry to *turn back the streams of war.*

In the early nineties, I was invited to sing at the World Peace Conference in Belfast before His Holiness the Dalai Lama and many politicians who had gathered from all over the world. I composed a special piece called '*Sí Gaoithe*' or 'Spirit Breeze' and was accompanied by a Mongolian throat singer called Michael Ormiston. Brigid felt near as I sang in the Irish language, calling in the wisdom of our ancestors with a message for peace and harmony between politicians and spiritual leaders of many traditions and faiths. Standing barefoot on a mound of earth that was part of the set design, I had a sense of how this woman can inform our heart and soul if we learn to open, trust and listen deeply to the power and the guidance of her message.

Brigid's cross inspired deep healing in later years between 1994 and 1997, when I travelled to Bosnia and Kosovo during the Balkan war. As a psychotherapist with the Dublin Rape Crisis Centre, a colleague and I were asked to travel to work with communities that had been traumatised by the war. Being in a country torn apart by conflict is an eye-opener and changes your perspective on life permanently. The landscape in both Balkan countries is beautiful and I was struck by the resilience of the people I met there. They spoke about the comfort they got from the changing seasons and a sense that the mountains had seen and known all that their broken hearts had experienced. They had lost their loved ones, homes and trust in all of life, as neighbours who had formerly lived side by side were now in conflict with each other. I often went to the island of Inis Mór on returning from these trips as a way to heal the memories in a calm and peaceful place.

On one occasion I travelled to Kosovo shortly after the Kildare celebration and ritual on Brigid's eve. The Brigidine sisters kindly gave woven crosses to bring to our groups. My colleague Angela and I were moved by their response to these messages of support from people in Ireland, who cared about them as they struggled to find ways of reconciliation and rebuild their lives. Brigid felt like a significant guide in our work there and was often invoked in a debriefing meditation and prayer held each evening. Connecting with her brought a sense of calm and support during very difficult and challenging times.

When we remember and celebrate the power of Brigid as an archetype, we can awaken to the beauty of all that draws our attention to new growth in our daily lives. Deep under the earth, seeds that germinated in darkened soil begin to stretch and pop their heads in early spring. Learning from the natural rhythm of nature and our friends the daffodils, let's cross this threshold, trusting in a new dawn of birth, creativity and hope.

Prayer to Saint Brigid

You were a woman of peace.
You brought harmony where there was conflict.
You brought light to the darkness.
You brought hope to the downcast.

May the mantle of your peace
cover those who are troubled and anxious,
and may peace be firmly rooted in our hearts
  and in our world.
Inspire us to act justly and to reverence
  all God has made.
Brigid you were a voice for the wounded
  and the weary.
Strengthen what is weak within us.
Calm us into a quietness that heals and listens.
May we grow each day into greater
wholeness in mind, body and spirit.
Amen.

– Solas Bhríde, Brigidine Sisters, Kildare

mary

Brigid, spread your mantle about us,
covering us with hope and harmony, joy and love.

– Traditional prayer to St Brigid

I have an icon of Brigid hanging in my kitchen and it certainly gives me a sense of hope, joy and love. There's a strength in her eyes and a gentleness in her demeanour. When I think of Brigid, the words that come to mind are: 'What a woman!' She is known for her generous spirit, her can-do attitude. She did found a monastery, after all! There's a brightness about her as she heralds the start of spring and with that a sense of light, hope, growth and rebirth, positive qualities of *Imbolg* that are especially welcome after the dark days of *Samhain*. Brigid has many patronages. She is beloved of the poor, of blacksmiths, beekeepers, brewers, singers, mothers and infants. What a wonderfully diverse and life-affirming portfolio for one person. Without doubt, it is her role as protector of mothers, of birth and babies that has kept me connected to Brigid since the allure of cleaning out her well at the bottom of our road in Clondalkin wore off, many years ago.

The hope and light I associate with Brigid has helped to keep my spirits up since my baby granddaughter, Holly, was born just before Christmas 2020, a second child for Eva and Benny and a little sister for Paddy. The logo on one of her babygros was very apt: 'I was born during a pandemic. I'll survive anything.' In years to come, she will be regaled with stories about being born in lockdown. We will remember and be thankful it's over. I was glad that Holly wasn't Eva's first baby because her antenatal and birth experiences were solitary for the most part. Her husband wasn't allowed to attend the antenatal visits and when she went into labour, he brought her to the hospital, waited in the car park until she was ready to deliver, at which stage he was allowed to be with her as their baby girl came into the world, a moment of huge joy, miraculous yet deeply natural and physical at the same time.

Two hours later, Benny left his wife and new baby in the care of the maternity hospital and the next time he saw them was when he returned to bring them home three days later.

Those were a lonely and emotional few days for both parents. They were very grateful, however, that this was not their first baby and that she was born healthy.

A new baby brings hope, love and a real sense of possibility into a family. This positive energy was very welcome when Holly was born during a lockdown that prevented her from being introduced to the extended family over Christmas and for months after that. We were all buoyed by her arrival, which provided a beacon of light during a dark time of isolation and separateness. I looked forward every day to hearing the ping on my phone that heralded a new batch of photos from Limerick. Eva and Benny did not disappoint. There were daily updates on how Holly slept and fed overnight and the cutest photos of her and Paddy.

My heart sang with love and connection and a feeling that we had wonderful moments to look forward to. I was grateful that both my grandchildren were really young during the pandemic and therefore the impact on them of being apart from family was less than if they had developed relationships and bonds with relatives that had to be broken. The loss was felt more keenly by the adult relatives, in fairness. The realisation that there were happy times ahead coincided with the advent of *Imbolg* on St Brigid's Day, 1 February, the first day of spring in the Celtic calendar.

Holly and Paddy have brought an extra vitality to our clan, a sense of belonging, of a continuum that has overcome the obstacles posed by the pandemic. When I think of them and the new life that they represent, the growth, the rebirth of our family, I'm reminded of Brigid and her qualities of connection, growth and positivity. She truly is a worthy icon, a herald of springtime in all its fertility, colour and joy. We are privileged to have her as a pivotal figure in our Celtic souls.

Deirdre and I are both blessed to have grown up with a respect for Brigid and how she can inform us to follow the heart, trusting in the turning of seasons and a celebration of new light and life. So, let us cross this threshold towards a new dawn of birth, creativity and hope.

dóchas: hope

In this cave of darkness
Breath carries the sound
Within the silence.
Held in the home of stones
Where bones of those
Whose song is sung
Still listen and re-sound.
To harmonise with all there was
And will be.
Echoing in cavities of tomb and womb,
Vibrations shudder at the hope
Of Birth and death.
The flow of morning
Song of soil and soul

In rhythm with
Contractions of the Earth.

– From 'Hope', *Celtic Passage*

deirdre

'*The flow of morning*' is a beautiful phrase that captures the movement of time as the sun rises each new day following the stillness and darkness of night. The Celtic communities lived so closely to the rhythm of the sun and seasons that each new day was a cause for celebration. Spring arrived and it was the dawn chorus of strengthening birdsong that called the farmers to prepare the soil for the planting of new seeds and the growing of crops that would nourish both body and soul.

In the Hebrides, it is said that the women curtsy and the men tip their caps in honour of the sun as it rises and sets each day. Circling the sun is also remembered when people make their journey *deiseal* or clockwise around the holy wells at times of pilgrimage or celebration of their local saint. Step by step with their hope and intention held firmly in their heart they listen deeply to the stirrings of their inner and outer worlds. What a wonderful way to notice the spiral of change that almost invites a dance and movement in rhythm and in tune with nature.

The symbol of the spiral has so often been exquisitely represented in the architecture, art and jewellery of the Celtic world.

It is also a symbol that is associated with the goddess Brigid, as the thread of life emerging from her and returning back again within for renewal. It represents the eternal energy of birth, death and rebirth and is a fitting symbol for our exploration of hope, having crossed this threshold of spring. That spiralling energy offers us a way of looking at our lives as movement from birth, growth, maturity, death and rebirth and in drawing from a deeper well, a journey of the soul, connecting us to all of life and its seasons.

Crossing these thresholds can offer us space to pause and reflect on times of hope in our own lives, or people who have inspired us with their journey of courage and vision, especially in situations of great adversity.

mary

The curtains parted to reveal a stage filled with children dressed in their traditional Russian costumes: the girls resplendent in red bonnets, white ruffled blouses and red pinafores; the boys handsome in their crisp white shirts, woven brown knee-length trousers and polished brown boots. To say these children were excited is a huge understatement. It was all they could do not to jump down from the stage to run to Debbie Deegan and smother her with hugs and kisses. Not before they sang their songs, however, played their instruments and performed the dances they had rehearsed to welcome the Irish people who had come to visit them at their home, Hortolova orphanage in Bryansk, almost 400 km southwest of Moscow, close to the border with Belarus.

Debbie is a Dublin mother who visited Hortolova in the late nineties and was so shocked by the conditions of the orphanage that she was determined to improve the lives of the children there. She didn't know how she was going to achieve this, but her heart would not allow her to leave them to their miserable fate. The Hortolova that Debbie encountered was a cold, grey, damp, multi-storied stone building. There were many broken windows, in a part of Russia that sees lows of minus 10 degrees in winter. The stench from the dark, unlit corridors was overwhelming because blown light bulbs were not replaced and the children were too frightened to walk to the toilet during the night. There was no joy in the lives of these little ones, living in an under-resourced setting, run by equally under-resourced staff.

When Debbie outlined her intention to take this orphanage under her wing, you'd have been forgiven for thinking this was a hopeless dream. We are talking about a place that's 2,000 km from Ireland, necessitates a flight to Moscow, a train journey to Bryansk and then a car trip to Hortolova, where nobody spoke English, where people lived in poverty, had their own problems and didn't concern themselves with the orphans.

Debbie was not for turning. She said from the beginning that the one thing she knew she could give these children was hope. This amazing Irish woman epitomises the qualities of the triple spiral: the regenerative power of female wisdom, experience, compassion and nurturing. She is a powerhouse of energy, positivity and love. The charity she founded, To

Russia with Love – now called To Children with Love – reflects these qualities and since 1998 has widened its remit to work with children in Ireland also.

Debbie was single-minded and part of her ingenuity was how she brought communities together to help. Predictably, the Irish people rose to the challenge, and have been very supportive. She persuaded the governor of Wheatfield prison to allow the inmates to build equipment for a playground in their woodwork classes. They were delighted to help out and that playground has been well used and loved by the children in Hortolova. It's on the right-hand side as you make your way up the driveway to the orphanage, which bears no resemblance to the cold, grey institution that greeted Debbie on her first visit. Once she received approval from the Russian authorities, she demolished that woebegone structure. In its place there's a welcoming communal building with classrooms, a dining area and the hall where that stage show at the beginning of this piece took place.

I visited Hortolova several times with Debbie, always in the spring, and those visits made me very proud of my fellow Irish woman. My first trip was about ten years after Debbie began her journey of love and hope. When our car pulled up outside the entrance hall, the children squealed with delight and ran to open the car door for their 'Mama'. They were happy, well-nourished and warmly dressed. Yes, it was springtime but that has a different connotation weather-wise in the heart of Russia! I noticed one little boy who remained apart from the crowd. He was pale, had sores on his lips and his hair was matted. His eyes were dull and he was quite taken aback by these scenes of exuberance. This all made sense when it was pointed out that he had been transferred from a neighbouring orphanage that morning. He didn't realise it at the time, poor lad, but this was his lucky day. And so it transpired.

By my second visit to Hortolova, to mark the publication of Debbie's book about her journey with the orphanage, that little boy was most definitely one of the family. He was taller, healthier and his eyes, once dull and trained on the ground, were sparkling and full of life. He had love in his life, he had fun and hope for the future, all thanks to the determination of one Irish woman.

Debbie Deegan's dedication has been all-consuming. She achieved her goal of bringing hope into the lives of unloved Russian children with the unwavering support of her husband and family. I returned to Hortolova with Debbie in 2018 and it was heart-warming to see young men and women who had grown up in the orphanage and achieved success in their lives. Debbie counts baristas, mechanics, doctors and lawyers among her Hortolova family. It was delightful to visit two former residents in an apartment block in Bryansk. These young women, both married with babies of their own, were adamant that their children would be loved and cared for, a far cry from the way they were brought up before Debbie's intervention changed the course of their lives.

Isn't that the way with the Celtic spiral? There's a continuum of that female power of nurturing. There are others who epitomise this powerful Celtic trait, dedicating their lives to looking after the needs of vulnerable people. Adi Roche is another good example. She founded Chernobyl

Children International (CCI) in the wake of the world's worst nuclear accident in Belarus in 1986. For more than thirty years now, she and her team have worked tirelessly to provide a home and love for children whose lives have been tragically affected by the disaster. I visited Vesnova with Adi and I was shocked by the utter devastation of the area. This poverty-stricken place is grey and depressing. The CCI compound stands out like a beacon of light, a sanctuary of hope in the midst of this gloom and doom. Here the colours are bright, the children are loved and cared for. Adi and her team work hard when they are there and also at home, raising money and awareness. Adi has addressed the UN General Assembly. She never stops speaking on behalf of the people of Belarus. All this work as chief executive of CCI and she takes no salary.

Sr Stanislaus Kennedy is in her eighties now and she is still speaking out on behalf of homeless people. She founded Focus Ireland and also the Immigrant Council of Ireland. Both organisations are part of the fabric of care in Ireland. Sr Stan is also aware of the need to promote awareness of our vulnerable neighbours among young people and to that end she founded Young Social Innovators (YSI), an initiative that allows Transition Year students to undertake projects with civic and humanitarian themes. YSI started small in 2001 but is now a mainstay of secondary education all around the country.

Deirdre and I began this part of our journey to the well of Celtic spirituality with a celebration of Brigid, source of the Divine Feminine in its wisdom, power, compassion and nurturing, qualities that have been passed on through the female line through the centuries and there's no doubt that these three women – Debbie Deegan, Adi Roche and Sr Stan – are the embodiment of the Divine Feminine today. The Celtic spiral emanates from their hearts and souls. There are many other examples of this spirit, which is part of our make-up as a Celtic people, women and men all around Ireland who go above and beyond for the sake of their families, their neighbours, their communities. We are lucky to have a tradition of concern for our fellow travellers along the road of life.

I encountered many examples of this wonderful quality during my years travelling the length and breadth of the country for RTÉ's *Nationwide*. Billy's Tearooms in Ballyhale in Kilkenny is a good example. The local people saw a need, particularly among their older neighbours, for a social outlet, so they got together and spent three years renovating a premises on Main Street and converting it into a welcoming cafe. It's run by the community for the community, staffed by volunteers, and the cakes and tarts are made by the community also. The tearooms have given a new vibrancy to a quiet village and enhanced the lives of the residents, who have somewhere to go for a cuppa now.

What motivated the people of Ballyhale was concern for their community. This is familiar to us in Ireland and I feel that we don't give ourselves enough credit for our highly developed sense of caring for other people. It's part of our DNA as Irish people, a great legacy of the tradition of nurturing that began thousands of years ago with our Celtic ancestors and which we remember whenever we speak of the Celtic spiral.

Is ar scáth a chéile a mhaireann na daoine.

We live in the shadow of each other.

– Traditional Irish saying

As Irish people, we need to acknowledge this gift that we possess. We go above and beyond to bring consolation and hope to those around us.

I remember a trip with *Nationwide* to Liberia to record a programme with the Irish peacekeepers serving with the United Nations. The Irish contingent was billeted in the former Hotel Africa. In their time off, the Irish men and women adopted two charities in the capital, Monrovia, helping to build an orphanage for children whose parents had been killed in the civil war and volunteering at a hospice, run by the Missionaries of Charity for people dying of AIDS. They looked around them when they arrived in that country, ravaged by war and poverty, saw the devastation and stood up to the plate as volunteers. Why? Because they wanted to help. They saw despair and they brought love, support and hope.

The story is similar in every corner of the world where there is need. That's where you will find the Irish – volunteering and giving hope in a very caring and selfless manner. I consider this to be an innate part of our make-up as Irish people. We need to recognise the positive impact we have and give ourselves credit for it. Too often our reaction when we are praised for an act of service is 'Sure it was nothing. Anyone would do the same.' Actually, that is not the case. We should give ourselves a collective pat on the back and be thankful that our ancestry has introduced us to this spiral of nurturing. Isn't it nice to think that our character as a nation includes this desire to improve the lives of others, bringing hope into hearts that are without it? There are people reading this book who may never have heard of the Celtic spiral but, just like the men and women in these pages, they have been touched by its essence and bring hope and love to the people they meet.

deirdre

Perhaps there are times when our own hearts are without hope, when the well runs dry and we are in need of courage to be present to our own vulnerability as human beings. We have spoken about our ancestors and their resilience in dealing with situations in the past, but it can be beneficial to explore what it is that sustains and brings a sense of hope during our own challenges and storms of the heart. The constant movement of the spiral reminds us that 'this too will pass', so being able to draw water from the well of our own resources can offer a sense of belonging to a spirit that moves in rhythm with the natural changing seasons from darkness into light. The core of contemplative life offers an invitation to be fully present to the reality of our experience, yet so often we live a life of disconnection from this reality, placing huge demands and expectations on ourselves and others. How would it be to pause at the empty well, kneel and, in meeting the reality of who and how we are, draw on ways that help us move forward with a feeling of renewed and realistic hope?

The arrival of *Imbolg* brings with it a new light, a longer day and a tapestry of colour and growth following the depths and harshness of winter. A single seed, warmed in the moist and darkened earth, soon stretches to become a new shoot, a new presence and a new possibility for further growth.

How might spring inform our journey as we take one step forward like a tiny seed, planted in the ever-unfolding spiral of our lives?

Courage

Search out your courage
Spiral of experience
In and around all that circles.

Wandering,
Through the landscape of the heart
Which opens wide to cradle you.

Search out your courage
Tiny seeds awaken …
Listening in the longing …
Tender lullaby of womb.

– Deirdre Ní Chinnéide

labyrinth

Is treise an dúchas ná an oiliúint.

Nature is stronger than learning.

– Traditional Irish saying

deirdre

On visiting many sites of Celtic tradition, it is not unusual to come across a meandering path woven in the ground where pilgrims walk mindfully around its long and winding pattern. A spiral path leads to a central core and back out again. Although you can feel as if you are walking around in circles, you eventually arrive at the centre, which then brings you back out to the point from which you started.

No one knows the origin of the labyrinth, but it spans many cultures and faiths. France's Chartres Cathedral holds the oldest known eleven-circuit pattern and, being indoors, pilgrims are allowed to walk on their knees if they so wish, to add an extra bit of variety to their journey.

Walking the labyrinth is symbolic of the journey we take in life and it is often used as a prayer or meditation, allowing us to quieten the mind and to mindfully walk and follow the various turns that eventually lead to the centre. It offers a lovely opportunity to take time to listen to the deeper stirrings of the heart at the various stages of our journey, one step at a time.

Nestled in the valley of Glendalough, a well-known monastic site in Wicklow, the labyrinth is cradled by the tall round tower and ancient ruins of the monastic city. The sound of the breeze swaying through the trees accompanies the pilgrim in the sacredness of this ancient and holy site. Who knows who walked this labyrinth over time, but there is no doubt that following this ritual provides a restful way of reflecting on the different experiences and chapters of our lives.

I have walked the labyrinth many times and am always surprised at an image, memory or feeling that might arise when time is given for a break away from the business of normal daily routine and schedules. I love to remember St Kevin as I wander through the labyrinth at Glendalough, recalling the story of how when he was at prayer one day, a bird landed on his outstretched hand and laid an egg. Kevin waited in prayer until the egg was hatched and the new fledglings were ready to fly, teaching the importance of patience and a deep relationship with the natural world.

Labyrinths are often found in places of great beauty and it was in one such place that Mary and I found ourselves unexpectedly walking its path together. It was a warm sunny day when we arranged to meet in Manresa, the Ignation Centre of Spirituality in Dublin. I had been part of a team facilitating a programme called Dóchas/Hope and was delighted to share an afternoon showing her around the place and meeting Fr Piaras Jackson SJ, the director of the retreat centre and the inspiration behind the building of a labyrinth in the beautiful grounds. It was nice to walk the labyrinth that day as sisters, and as we made our way around the spiral path, I had a sense of us both sharing a journey that began on a similar road, but which subsequently brought quite diverse experiences to our lives. We both began our working lives as teachers, both married and divorced and both ended up in totally different careers and family experiences. Even so, here we were, not knowing what the labyrinth was opening for either of us but walking in silence through our shared and separate experiences on the journey of life.

Manresa has been a great support in my life and I have spent time there on week-long silent retreats. They are a wonderful opportunity, especially during threshold times, to spend time in silence and to draw from the deeper well. On one such occasion, struggling with a challenge of great uncertainty and transition in my life, the labyrinth became a daily part of a prayer and meditation and it was so interesting to see how each time could bring a different insight and sense of direction.

Pausing to reflect during times of transition and change

brings with it a possibility to move forward with a sense of letting go of the old, while embracing all that stepping forward into a new direction brings.

It can call for a great leap of faith, as you let go of the security and familiarity of a way of life, stepping into total mystery as to where the new path might lead. So often this spiralling can feel like going around in circles, but in fact clarity usually settles after a while into a new paradigm and the unfolding of a new chapter.

There is a labyrinth, created in recent years, on the eastern side of the island of Inis Mór, but in many ways the whole island is like a labyrinth as you wander around its meandering roadways. They say that the island calls to the soul and if that happens you might find yourself staying longer than you had initially planned. That was certainly my experience and when I lived in Dublin, the island was a great place to visit to reflect on some major transitions or challenges in life. It always felt like a safe holding place, where I could come and take a little time away from life on the mainland with its demands and responsibilities. That is why retreats work really well here. People come to take time for renewal; they drink from the waters of their own inner holy well and return refreshed and ready to take on whatever changes are calling for attention.

It isn't always an easy road but as Mary now highlights, when we trust the calling that is urging us to listen, it can bring new insights and a sense of walking a deeper journey of the heart.

mary

It had been a difficult few months prior to that sunny day when Deirdre and I walked the labyrinth in Manresa. It was during the pandemic and Ireland had been in lockdown for a couple of months, from the end of March until July. Like everybody else, we had battened down the hatches and lived quietly within a 2, then 5, then 20 km radius of our homes. Normally, we would see each other fairly regularly during the year but, like everyone else, we accepted the greater purpose of this way of living. Deirdre turned sixty at the end of March and we had planned a big party. Instead, the family raised a glass to her via Zoom, our hotel-break plans put to one side, for now. That afternoon walk around the labyrinth in the grounds of the Manresa retreat centre was all the more cherished for it.

It was my first time to visit this peaceful, graceful centre close to the sea in Clontarf in Dublin. The grounds are expansive, with tall trees and a lush lawn containing the labyrinth. Deirdre led the way. I was very aware of the importance from ancient times of this path for Celtic people and I felt as if we were walking in the footsteps of our ancestors as we set out at a slow, meandering pace from the entrance through the winding path, until eventually we reached the centre. There's a consolation knowing that there are no dead ends in a labyrinth, just turns along the way. You are always on the right path and if you continue on this single walkway, you will definitely reach the centre. Certainly, our Celtic ancestors did well to incorporate the labyrinth into their thinking and their way of life. They have presented us with an opportunity to walk its path as a metaphor for life's journey and a chance to reflect on our own lives.

As I reflected on this reunion with Deirdre, I thought back to our common upbringing and our individuality. As Deirdre said, our lives went in different directions and yet here we were, on a sunny afternoon, walking together on a single path towards a single centre. I felt quite apart from the outside world as I looked into my heart and let my thoughts and feelings speak to me, of family, of sisterhood, of relationships. The timing of this encounter contributed to the strength of those feelings. There's nothing like being apart from loved ones to make us appreciate what we have. Like so many, lockdown granted me lots of time to evaluate priorities and recognise the important things in life. Things like being able to hug, to hold, to have people around my table, to party, to laugh and cry together, rather than through the lens of a phone or laptop.

I remembered good times that Deirdre and I had shared. Our mother celebrated her eightieth birthday on Inis Mór. The three of us stayed in Deirdre's house and on 22 June, we hiked to the top of Dún Aonghasa, the largest of the prehistoric stone forts on the Aran Islands. It's a 100 m climb to the top and Mam was in step with the rest of us. No mean achievement for a woman of eighty, and she was understandably proud. She certainly cemented her Celtic credentials on that day. My heart was bursting with love and a sense of belonging to these two women. It felt very special and spiritual. There was a primal connection between this mother and her two daughters, to be held in a special place in our hearts, especially as Mam was diagnosed with cancer within twelve months and died three years later.

My thoughts then drifted to my own daughters, Eva and Lucy, and their connection to me, their mother, and to Deirdre, their aunt. The bond is strong and loving and for that I am grateful. We have had some good times together. A few days before Eva was married, I booked a night away with her and Lucy in a Dublin hotel, a chance to get some head space away from lists and dresses, cakes and flowers. We had a great night and were joined for dinner, drinks and a lot of laughs by Deirdre, my sister-in-law Eileen and her daughter, Clare. Clare and Lucy were Eva's bridesmaids. All agreed that this simple gathering was a very special memory from the first wedding in the family. It was a celebration of the female line and a reminder of the importance of that sisterhood across the generations.

I do not take for granted the richness that a simple walk in a labyrinth brought into my consciousness. Deirdre and I walked slowly and mindfully and I truly feel that I journeyed to the well of family memory deep in my heart as I walked. What emerged was a feeling of rebirth as I made it to the centre of the labyrinth. I felt a renewed connection to my Celtic roots and the ancient culture from which my memory derives and a huge appreciation and gratitude for the gift of good women in my life.

deirdre and mary

When we take time to walk mindfully through the roads that have unfolded in our lives, we can feel a strong link with the story that has gone before us. Who are our people, our tribe, not just on a personal level but as a country firmly built on Celtic roots? Imagine getting an aerial view of the labyrinth as a symbol of your life, linking back to generations that went before and seeing your place in the fabric of that story.

There is, of course, the challenge of finding skeletons in the cupboard, but also a huge potential to become aware of the healing of these stories, being conscious of what we want to change and cherish in passing on to the next generation.

Every year we gather as an extended family to remember our mam and dad on 23 December, which was the day that Mam died in 2001. It certainly marked that Christmas with great sorrow and loss. In time, however, and with healing, it has become a day that brings us all together to celebrate and remember the gift of who they were and the extended family that grew from their love. They couldn't have known at the centre of the labyrinth of their lives that many years later there would be children and grandchildren that still gather in gratitude, recounting stories and memories that keep them alive in our hearts.

It is delightful now to include the next generation with Paddy and Holly and in years to come the room will hopefully fill with little ones on their way to becoming part of the continuation of the family line and labyrinth.

One of the greatest gifts we will both always cherish from the pandemic is a handprint of Paddy's sent to all of us by Eva, following his first adventure with paint. The poem penned by his mam would bring tears to your eyes but released emotions of love and longing to reconnect and enjoy the support of family.

> *There was a young boy called Paddy,*
> *Who sometimes got very saddy*
> *Family he did miss*
> *Couldn't give them a kiss,*
> *So he sent them a wave of his handy.*

This generational ritual of walking the labyrinth is like turning the pages of the story of our lives. There are twists and turns that open up to a new road we hadn't noticed or expected along the way. While we may have had clear plans and expectations for how our life would develop, in hindsight perhaps things have unfolded differently. Taking time to reflect on the challenges met and gifts received along the way provides a deeper way of connecting to the turning points of our labyrinth that continues to unfold as we develop and grow.

Labyrinths are now being built in public places like hospitals, hospices, outdoor gardens and even schools, a chance for people to slow down and walk mindfully, which is especially helpful if they are dealing with adverse situations in life.

In recent times, we have all been faced with a myriad of feelings that may have been distressing and difficult to deal with. Walking the labyrinth can offer a little time to meander through its path and return to a quietened mind. Even if it is not possible to find a labyrinth in your locality, you can have an experience of this wonderful ritual by tracing your finger on the labyrinth on page 83.

The Celts believed in a thin veil between this world and the spirit world or the land of the *Sí* (faery folk). Opening to other realms of reality brings in the connection between our own lives and the spirit and blessing of our ancestors. When we take time to reflect on our own story and that which has gone before us, we can feel less alone and trust in the presence and guidance of others who have walked this way.

It's good to travel slowly so that you feel a connection to the sense of journey, moving through the pathway that makes up the gift and story of who you are.

Become aware of any images, emotions, memories or body sensations that you experience as you make your way around the labyrinth, remembering that there are always new ways ahead, possibilities and opportunities to move through times of uncertainty and to cross a threshold towards hope.

Bean Sí

In the call of the wind
There is Bean sí
Woman of women
Who beckons to a land
Where trees sway around her.
Leaves a garment
Flickering their light,

Curtesy to a natural fall.
And walking barefoot
On a path to paths
Unknown
She branches out.

– From 'Wisdom Woman',
Deirdre Ní Chinnéide

a spiral labyrinth

Using your index finger on your non-dominant hand, take a few deep breaths and begin from the outside, tracing the meandering path that will eventually bring you into the centre. Pause for a moment in the centre and after taking a few more deep breaths, trace your journey back out to the place from where you began.

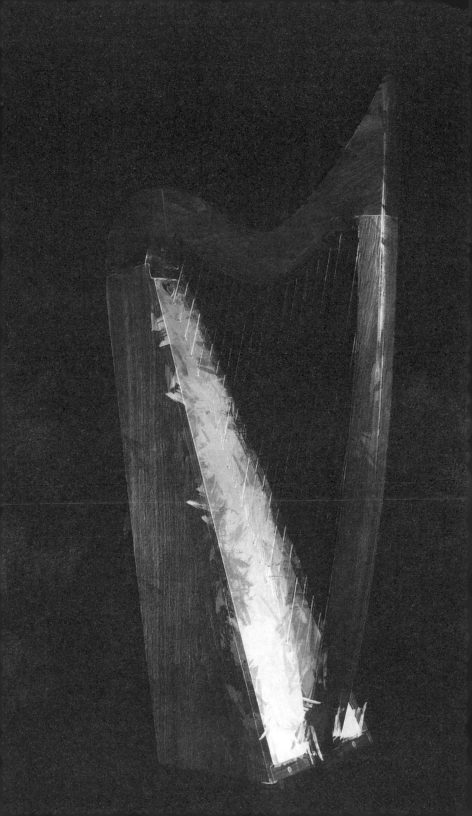

the harp

'Sí Gaoithe' ('Spirit Breeze')
Hear the song
That sings through Stone.
Sí Gaoithe,
Lulls its children Home.

deirdre

In Celtic mythology, Dagda, known as the Good God of all Gaelic Gods, was the King of the Tuatha De Danann, the faery folk, who it is said lived in the otherworld of a supernatural nature. Dagda had a magical harp that travelled everywhere with him and would even answer and respond to his call. His music was enchanting – made up of three types of melodies: the *goltraí* or lament; the *geanntraí*, which brought great joy to the listener; and the *suantraí* or lullaby, which was used to lull people into a sound and restful sleep. We in Ireland are known for our gift of music and the ability to carry our story in song and melody has travelled and enchanted the world. The notes of the harp can transport us to mystical realms of great soothing, sorrow and joy, enticing the imagination into the land of the *Sí*, or faery folk.

It is said that music from the land of the *Sí* can be heard lilting through the strings of the harp as the breeze blows an enchanted melody. Music was considered a fifth element of the Celtic world along with air, fire, water and earth, a healing balm that could nourish and renew the soul. Our Celtic music unites us with other nations, a language that crosses many boundaries and offers hope, happiness and healing.

In this chapter we honour the harp as a symbol that stands for the Irish nation, an instrument of exquisite beauty and a doorway that opens a heartfelt connection to a deep well of music with its roots in the melodic strains of the ever ancient and evolving Celtic world.

mary

The harp that once through Tara's halls
the soul of music shed,
now hangs as mute on Tara's walls

as if the soul were fled.

– From 'The Harp That Once Through Tara's Halls'

The feeling of sadness and despair in those lines from Thomas Moore's famous melody, written while Ireland was still under English rule, have long since been replaced by a feeling of joy and exuberance whenever the Irish harp is played. Add to that the patriotic pride the harp evokes. It's our national symbol, the identifying mark of the presidential seal, of government documents, of our passports. It's even the emblem of the iconic pint of Guinness!

The Irish harp is smaller and played differently to the classical harp, but it punches way above its weight and takes centre stage in springtime, as we celebrate our national holiday, St Patrick's Day. The traditions of St Patrick's Day are legion, celebrated around the world in modern times. We witness the Eiffel Tower, the Sydney Opera House or the Colosseum going green for the day, and can feel proud of our international reputation.

I am known for decorating my house on special occasions and Lá Fhéile Pádraig is definitely one of them. Down from the attic come shamrock-shaped paper chains, the leprechaun ornaments, the green candles and the rest of the paraphernalia made by my children when they were in junior school and which they plead with me every year to consign to the dustbin. I'm far too sentimental for that and I remember with love and fondness their excitement as they would run out the school gate to present me with their personally crafted card or token. Those treasures won't be leaving my collection any time soon. In fact, the decorations that I and my brothers and sister made for my mother when we were children were only thrown out after she died. We reckoned it was the turn of our children, the next generation, to have their moment in the sun and their works of art adorning our houses. There's a continuity to this practice that indicates for me the generational flow in my family, a reminder that we belong to each other and that the childlike recognition of our national day combines very nicely with the more adult version.

I always loved St Patrick's Day as a child and would float to mass that morning on a cloud of wellbeing, feeling gorgeous thanks to the green satin ribbon in my hair and very proud because of the sprig of shamrock pinned to my Patrick's Day badge with the gold foil harp in the centre. I would belt out the words of the hymn:

> *Hail glorious Saint Patrick, dear saint of our isle,*
> *On us, thy poor children, bestow a sweet smile,*
> *And now thou art high in the mansions above,*
> *On Erin's green valleys, look down in thy love.*

Mass was followed by a quick dash home to eat some of the sweets that had been saved in a box. I always gave up sweets for Lent, but they were in scarce enough supply in those days so any sweet that came my way was put into a tin box, to be eaten at the end of Lent or on St Patrick's Day, which offered a dispensation. Those were the nicest sweets ever, a mixture of wrapped and unwrapped, boiled, chocolate, hard, soft. The fact that they all tasted the same, having shared that tin for weeks, mattered not a whit. They were flavourlicious! And all the sweeter for the lack of them for weeks.

We always went into Dublin city to the parade, a far simpler affair than today's event. I remember a particular security company seemed to be the only group to have money to do up a float in those days. It was a series of marching bands and dancing schools and we would reserve our loudest cheer for our own St Joseph's Pipe Band from Clondalkin. The band was founded in 1937 and many is the night I went to sleep as a youngster listening to them practising in the Round Towers GAA club around the corner from St Brigid's Road, where we lived. They continue to grace all Clondalkin occasions, and have gone from strength to strength, having won the World Pipe Band Championships in Glasgow in 2019.

Clondalkin has its own St Patrick's Day parade now. As luck would have it, the route passes our old family home and when my children and their cousins were small, we would take them to their granny's house and sit them on her garden wall to wave their flags and watch the parade go by. I have a lovely photo of them in their green finery, waving and cheering their hearts out! Fast forward to St Patrick's Day 2016, when I was honoured to be grand marshal of the Clondalkin parade, a special celebration of the centenary of the Easter Rising. The highlight for me was passing by 31 St Brigid's Road and seeing my adult children and their cousins on the wall of my childhood home. They had recreated the old photograph by lining up in the same sequence. Once again, they were waving for all they were worth, a wonderful gesture of support for me and their community and a reminder of the strength of family ties.

My final St Patrick's Day broadcast for *Nationwide* brought me to Banwen in Wales, reputed to be the birthplace of Patrick and the place where he was kidnapped and taken to Ireland as a young boy. This tiny little village is very proud of its connections to the saint. We filmed in the primary school and the children sang their song to St Patrick in Welsh. There's a plaque to St Patrick in the village and they, too, have their parade every year. It was really lovely to share stories with them and, in particular, to spend time in the classroom with the children and to see their projects celebrating St Patrick, a wonderful connection and a realisation of how much we share as Celtic people.

By St Patrick's Day on 17 March, *Imbolg* is well underway. The weather is getting warmer, the crops are being sown, the grass is growing. St Patrick's Day was traditionally the day the lawn got its first cut.

Ireland's third patron saint, St Colmcille (or St Columba) – is credited with bringing Christianity to Scotland and is buried on the island of Iona. St Brigid, St Patrick and St Colmcille are strong characters whose qualities subtly inform our sense of national identity. All three looked outside of themselves to support and improve the lives of people they encountered, bringing hope and a sense of community everywhere they went.

Some years ago, I travelled to Africa to make a St Patrick's Day programme for *Nationwide* about the Irish peacekeeping forces in Chad and the welcome we received was phenomenal. They were delighted to show us around and for us to bring greetings to their families in Ireland to be aired on national television. Here were Irish men and women looking after the needs of the local people, giving them support and hope in a very volatile part of the world. They went above and beyond the call of duty on many occasions, looking out for the vulnerable in this arid and rural part of Chad. They did their country and their uniform proud. The harps on their buttons were shining brightly, both literally and metaphorically.

The harp as a musical instrument produces notes that are light, melodic and deeply evocative of varying emotions from lament to celebration. The object itself is a thing of beauty, skilfully wrought from wood with flowing shapes and curves. It is an intrinsic reminder of our Celtic roots and evokes pride in our national identity, and for the high regard in which we are held in other parts of the world. The association between the harp and our national day represents hope and our wish is that that this national pride should spur us on to consider with compassion people and situations that need some love, dignity and respect from others in their lives. May we walk in the footsteps of St Patrick, imbued with the spirit of the peacekeepers in Chad, and may we give hope to others that we meet along the way.

Dóchas linn, Naomh Pádraig,
Aspal mór na hÉireann.

Bring us hope, St Patrick.
The great apostle of Ireland.

new dawn

Arise My Love my beautiful one,
Sí Gaoithe na hoíche
Éist leis an bhfonn,
A ardófar an duarchas a líonn ort go trom
Is a glaofor do Anam thar muir is thar tonn

Listen to the call that releases from darkness and
calls the soul over land and sea
to a love that dances and is free

– 'Arise my love', Celtic Passage

deirdre

With a deep connection to the sense of being firmly rooted in the natural world, we are called to listen to the sound of the breeze. *Sí Gaoithe* or spirit breeze, gently gestures to a new dawn of hope, courage and stability.

Spring equinox, celebrated on the eve of 20 March, marks a threshold when the day and night are of equal length. Spring arrives with a vibrancy of new life, growth and longer days. Nestled in the heart of this season is the celebration of Easter, named after the northern goddess Eostre, which later inspired the Christian festival.

John Moriarty, a well-known scholar from Ireland, who sadly passed away a couple of years ago, spoke about us being an Easter people, always in search of resurrection. I had the pleasure of spending time with John many times in his home nestled under Mangerton mountain in Co. Kerry. Our conversations would move from the sacred to the profane and I remember one day sitting from morning till night by his fireside, sorting out the problems of the world and passionately sharing our love and interest in faith and spirituality. John lived close to the land and eloquently spoke about the landscape as a woman, a goddess of Ireland, birthing food for us to eat and holding stories in her mountains, rivers and trees. I was reminded of the women of Kosovo during my work there following the Balkan war, who felt that in spite of the injustice they had experienced, the mountains had seen and heard everything. It speaks of a relationship with the land that is powerful and significant.

In Lubinich, a small village of 300 inhabitants, I met a woman called Maria who had lost five members of her family on 25 May 1999. Soldiers came and shot the men and young boys from this town, leaving the village in deep trauma and grief that will take generations to heal. As I shook Maria's hand, I could feel that she herself was hardly alive, with the grief of losing her loved ones. On my return to the Aran Islands following this journey, my own grief for her and what I had witnessed came to the surface on a day I walked quietly during Holy Week. I found myself drawn to the oldest church on the island and as I stood in front of the image of the pietà, one of the Stations of the Cross, the tears came flooding and I howled uncontrollably. There was something about releasing these tears that cracked open my heart and as Leonard Cohen beautifully reminds us, *that's where the light gets in – that's where the light gets in ...*

Easter is one of my favourite times of the year. Mary remembers as a child tucking in to her sticky sweet box on St Patrick's Day – the time of Lenten reprieve – and I can recall the delight we shared when Easter Sunday finally arrived and we had full freedom to devour all of our sweets, including chocolate eggs! There was always a feeling of lightness following the silence and sombre journey through Holy Week. The rituals were unusual and dramatic, and they brought various feelings of terror at a bloodstained crucifix, exhaustion at standing for a very long time while the longer gospel was read and delight that the week ended with good news and a celebration. My love of Easter has thankfully deepened during my life and it has become a very beautiful opportunity to walk through this message from darkness into light.

Spring mirrors this journey after we have travelled through the depths of winter and it's as if all of the natural world is responding with gratitude and celebration. My eighty-four-year-old neighbour Bearcla Winnie has lived on the island all of his life. He is a good and kind man with a twinkle in his eye, a great sense of humour and a love of building leprechaun houses – which he strategically places in his garden so that the tourists will believe that the faery folk are alive and well in Kilmurvey.

Many a time he has come to sit by the range of my house, chatting about his life long ago and the changes he has seen over the years. I love his sense of fun and his stories. A reporter asked him once how he managed to cope with the dark winters on the island. 'Sure, I watch *Judge Judy*,' he said, much to the delight of all those present. His kindness and care extends to his animals and the land itself and many a time he and his brother-in-law Laurence gave me help to build some raised beds for vegetables. I certainly would not claim to be an avid gardener like Mary, but I was willing to have a go and was fascinated by Bearcla's suggestion that we plant our seeds on Good Friday, assured that they will rise well, as the Easter story reminds us. Such connection to nature speaks of a lived experience of new beginnings of hope and growth.

At Easter, Inis Mór is at its best, with wildflowers carpeting the craggy rock and a knowledge that the new season will bring visitors from far and wide. One of my favourite evenings is Holy Thursday, where a silent prayer service is held as people come and visit the three churches on the island, which are beautifully decorated with candles and flowers. It is magical to leave at midnight and walk home under the dome of a star-studded sky.

I love when the family comes at Easter to enjoy the various rituals of music, dance, dawn mass and an egg hunt. It feels as if we all breathe a sigh of relief at the arrival of a new season with longer days and possibilities. One of the rituals that has developed in recent years on the island is a silent walk to the fort of Dún Aonghasa. People gather just as the new light of dawn is stretching and, with torch and candlelight, we walk to the top of the cliffs. On arrival we take time to wander around the fort and then gather to send out prayers and blessings to people who have emigrated, who are sick or are struggling with darkness in their lives. It is a lovely way to link into the spirit of a community gathering at this ancient place and to carry on the tradition and ritual of connecting to the ancestors who were here before us. Poems are read in Irish, written by acclaimed writers like Liam Ó Flaithearta or Máirtín Ó Direáin, who lived on the island long ago. The highlight is listening to a *sean nós* song sung by a local man, which fills us all with reverence for the language and culture of a people who captured deep feeling in the story of their songs.

I remember one year, when I was asked to scatter the ashes of a woman who had been on retreat with me on the island many years ago. It seemed like a strange request at first, but a beautiful experience to be part of a circle of islanders praying for her and her family and laying her ashes in a place that had spoken deeply to her soul. Another occasion that comes to mind was a gathering of retreatants from all over the world who had come to the island from the Edmund Rice Foundation. They were from India, Africa, Central America, South America, Cuba and Ireland. As we formed a circle, each person prayed in their native or tribal tongue. I had such an incredible sense of the power of this small island with a deep spirituality that connects to far corners of the world. I love the walk to Dún Aonghasa – it's almost like a pilgrimage of nations, where each person takes one step at a time to reach this threshold and stand in awe and wonder at the beauty and power of creation. The Celts believed that outdoors was the best place to worship their god, as no building could adequately house the immensity of such a presence.

Across on the mainland on Good Friday, such a tradition is followed by the walking of the Stations of the Cross outdoors in the valley of Maimean. Hundreds of people gather to be led up the mountain by the renowned Fr MacGreil, stopping at each of the Stations carved out in the landscape, offering a profound experience in the embrace of the majestic mountains. If my friend John Moriarty were still alive, he might describe the global pandemic as a Good Friday experience, bringing us all to a pause and the need for reflection.

How do we negotiate these harder times in our lives and find the resources and faith to cross these thresholds with hope of a new beginning? Being so close to nature and including ritual in daily life, the Celtic Christian story offers a chance to bless each movement through the darkness and through the light.

mary

There is no doubt that we, as Irish people, are close to nature. We live on an island, nobody is further than 85 km from the sea and for those who must travel that distance, there is the reward of passing through lush green countryside. This proximity to nature is part of our reality and it's often only when somebody from a much larger and more densely populated part of the world comments on the fact that you can get from the capital city to the coast or the mountains in about thirty minutes that it dawns on us how lucky we are. It's a privilege to be surrounded by elements of the natural world and I believe that, deep down, it informs our personalities and our attitudes to life. We are grounded as a people, we are curious, we are interested in the lives of others, we care.

If the pandemic is, as Deirdre's late friend John Moriarty might have described it, our Good Friday, the compassion, support and love felt for those who suffered in its wake mirrors those same qualities shown to Jesus along the route to Calvary and at the foot of the cross.

The Celtic traditions that accompanied that ritual during Holy Week were very much a part of our Easter, growing up in the sixties. Bearcla Winnie is an example of so many people in rural Ireland who insisted on sowing on Good Friday, in recognition of the Resurrection that would follow, ensuring that those plants would grow strongly, not three days after they were planted, obviously, but in the fullness of time. We have spoken of holy wells before. In former times, people collected their waters on Good Friday because tradition held that the waters were blessed with healing powers on that day. They also painted a cross for the Crucifixion on eggs laid on Good Friday and, as children, we ate hot cross buns that day. They were delicious and the highlight of an otherwise grim day. Truth be told, Holy Week was pretty grim from start to finish. But what a glorious finish awaited us on Easter Sunday.

Navigating Holy Week demanded resilience and a positive attitude for sure. We got our school holidays on Spy Wednesday when, as well as polishing desks and inkwells in the classroom, we would brace ourselves for the church ceremonies and the spring-clean.

Spy Wednesday, Maundy Thursday and Good Friday were marked by several church ceremonies, which had to be fitted in around the cleaning chores at home. Every house in Ireland was deep-cleaned over those few days and there were no cleaning companies that could be enlisted to ease the process. The cleaners were the children of the house, who all had their designated duties.

Deirdre and I washed the windows. Inside and out. That took time, I can tell you, and involved a lot of stretching, elbow grease and a certain amount of athleticism when it came to washing the outside of the upstairs bedroom windows. I remember hanging out the window and was even known to balance one leg on the windowsill. That was in the days before Health and Safety!

Our brothers and our dad would tackle the garden and the garage. Even the shed had to be sparkling for Easter. Mam did a lot of baking during Holy Week. Not that we got to taste any of it before Easter Sunday. The week was one of hardcore fasting, simple food and then on Good Friday, one meal and two 'collations'. I'm still not sure where the word came from but I do know what it meant: very little to eat! Is it any wonder that the hot cross buns were an absolute highlight.

Finally, Easter Sunday arrived and I will never forget the excitement of being given brand-new snow-white ankle socks that morning. I was delighted to see the back of the thick woollen socks for a few months and the fact that I was probably freezing on occasion until summer properly arrived didn't bother me at all. I thought I was the bee's knees and the cat's pyjamas walking to mass on Easter Sunday in a new dress and those ankle socks. The green hair ribbon on St Patrick's Day was only in the ha'penny place by comparison.

New clothes for the children of the house were very much part of our Irish traditions around Easter. Something to look forward to after the trials of Holy Week: the housework, the lengthy church ceremonies and the darkness of Good Friday. All over Ireland pubs remained closed on Good Friday, shops locked their doors and the TV went dark at three o'clock, the time of the Crucifixion, and the rest of the day's programming was of a solemn, religious type. The contrast between Holy Week and Easter Sunday was very clearly defined and there was a joy, a lightness that Deirdre referred to earlier, in that journey from the darkness into the light.

The lines are less clearly defined between the week and Easter Sunday in our modern, more secular times, but there is nonetheless a positive and hope-filled association that comes with Easter and the promise of warm sunny days ahead.

Deirdre spoke of our family spending Easter weekends on Inis Mór, punctuated by egg hunts, sea swims, the drama of the midnight Easter Vigil with its Paschal Fire in the churchyard and lovely food shared around her table. We have carried forward the torch handed to us by our parents, creating new family traditions for the next generation, a lot more appealing than the traditions of spring-cleaning and fasting that Deirdre and I knew growing up.

Such Easter observances bring us joy and light. We can be imbued with a sense of hope and a recognition that the way we live our lives, and the habits and traditions that we practise, define us as a people of considered values, formed and refined from times past by our ancestors, who travelled this road before us and handed down to us a rich Celtic heritage.

Our threshold has brought us into the belly of *Imbolg*, and all that springs from her is before us. With a lighter step, we have gathered under Brigid's cloak, spiralling through the labyrinth of our own stories and those of our ancestors. *Dóchas* (hope) has lit a path through the tradition of Patrick and the journey and celebration of Easter. With a sense of new dawn rising, we invite you to cross another threshold into a stronger experience of a bright and warm welcoming light.

Dawn

I will plant a garden
Watered by the moon.
Newborn leaves

Trembling through the night
Inhale their calling.
Come little ones
And sing the chorus
Of the winking Dawn
Stretching to its wake.

– Deirdre Ní Chinnéide

bealtaine

Bright Fire of Summer

introduction

Tabhair dom do lámh, a stoirín,
Tabhair dom do lámh, a ghrá
Tabhair dom do lámh, a stoirín
Is tabharfaidh mé duit an lá.

Give me your hand, my loved one,
Give me your hand in this way
Give me your hand, my loved one
Let's welcome the gift of the day.

– From '*Tabhair dom do lámh*'

deirdre

There is a light and bright melody to this chant that is often sung in a group as people dance and skip in a circle, weaving around each person they meet along the way. I have shared it with many groups around the world and it is a delight to see the joy and energy that comes from such a simple gesture.

It is typical of the song and dance of the maypole, celebrating the arrival at *Bealtaine* and crossing the threshold into the full light and abundance of summer. Swallows return from their winter in faraway lands, the sound of the cuckoo is heard and all of nature seems to spread her mantle like a newly worn garment of beauty and growth.

Our female deity is ripe with maturity and proudly watches over all that is emerging from the moist earth. In times gone by, our Celtic ancestors would have marked this season transition with great tradition and respect for how nature was responding to their needs. Gratitude was expressed through prayer, folklore and ritual, with honour and reverence for all that was being provided at this time.

Bealtaine, which falls on 1 May, rests strategically between the spring equinox of 20 March and the summer solstice of 21 June, the longest day of the year. Rituals marking this time were strongly connected to the changes that were happening in the natural world.

Bealtaine translates as 'bright fire', and these were duly lit all over the country as a symbol of crossing this threshold time. In the centre of Ireland is the legendary mythological site called Uisneach and in ancient times the Druids considered it to be the spiritual centre of the whole land. A great fire was lit on the hill of Uisneach by the High King of Ireland, symbolising the regeneration and rejuvenation of the earth after the long dark months of winter.

The fire was a symbol of purification and people gathered and danced over and around it in celebration of this time of growth and renewal. Crossing the fire was seen to bring protection, fertility and good luck and livestock might be walked between two lit fires as a blessing for the food they would provide for their owners and the community.

At the closing of the ritual, which often lasted till the sun rose the next morning, embers from the fire were placed as a blessing on the land and also brought to the hearth of the home. *Máthair tine* (mother fire) is a name given to this fire and is a lovely way of linking to the sacredness of fire and the almost umbilical connection to Mother Nature in all her fullness and growth.

Our *Brat Bhríde* ritual, placing a cloth outside the night before Brigid's Day in spring or *Imbolg*, was a way of gathering a dew blessing from the goddess as she swept over the land before the arrival of spring. We can see a connection to this ritual again in May, when the dew of *Bealtaine* brought healing and blessing for people who gathered and sprinkled it on crops, animals and their families. It was meant to give a great complexion and probably had anti-wrinkle properties and a promise of eternal youth! All in all, this time brought a feeling of joy, creativity, new life and hope.

So, let us journey to this well and drink of its healing waters through music, dance and the constant invitation to walk and connect with the sacredness and potential of who we are and can be, in the expression of our full and shining bright light.

The core of Celtic spirituality lies in its connection to and celebration of creation, and summer brings with it a sense of outdoor worship as all of life is sacramentally welcomed and adorned. No words are needed, but the eye can see and the ear can hear the symphony of sound in a dawn chorus of a new song.

All over Inis Mór, gentian, orchids, bluebells, daisies and cowslips shimmer in the once-barren limestone and the earth releases carpets of glorious colour on the canvas of *Bealtaine* beauty. Early morning is the best time to walk the boreens and at times you can feel like a visitor in the natural world, as you are greeted by newborn calves staying close to their mums but curiously watching your movements as you pass, and you witness birds, bees and animals getting along with their daily activities.

Wild garlic, leeks, berries, seaweeds and elderflowers are gathered and transformed into delicious food and brought to the kitchen table to accompany the spuds and vegetables that grow abundantly in the sandy Aran soil. There's a feeling of joy in the air, with strong and healthy geraniums adorning the newly whitewashed windowsills, and the whoops and hollers of swimmers can be heard from beaches on the long silent and starry nights.

I love when family and friends come to visit during the summer and delight in seeing them slowly begin to unwind and appreciate the gift that the island has to offer in a gentle break away from what can feel like another world entirely.

There is always a big interest in coming to visit 'Aunty Deirdre' for the celebration of St John's Eve on 23 June. It is a special night when fires are lit in each of the fourteen villages and the community gathers with food, drink, music and dance, often till sunrise the following morning. There is a bit of healthy competition between the different villages in relation to the biggest and best fire and often people take a trip around the island to get a look at what the neighbours are creating and how high their fire is!

It's a strong tradition that links back to the celebration that our ancestors would have had to mark the arrival of the summer solstice and thankfully it is still alive and well here on the island. It's a great way to meet the neighbours outdoors and the old couches and chairs that provide welcome seating during the event are eventually thrown onto the fire as the party ends and burned along with lots of other items that have been cleared from local garages and storehouses. I'm not sure St John and his community would have had the same level of luxury or partied in the same way, but I have no doubt that he is smiling somewhere at his feast day being remembered still.

The marking of these feast days through the summer months brings the islanders to the holy wells and sacred sites with prayer and worship in wonderful remembrance and respect for the spirit and life of those who have lived here through generations. Like their ancestors, the people live closely to the land and sea, respecting that interdependence with nature and all that the natural world provides.

Imagine the song of summer, where we could hum with the bees, dance with memory and bow in gratitude for the plants and animals that provide us with great abundance of pleasure and food. Perhaps then we could sing in harmony celebrating this new and vibrant season ...

mary

Samhradh, samhradh, bainne na ngamhna,
Thugamar féin an samhradh linn.
Samhradh buí na nóiní glégeal,
Thugamar féin an samhradh linn.

Summer, summer, milk of the calves,
We have brought the summer in.
Yellow summer of clear, bright daisies,
We have brought the summer in.

— From 'Samhradh, Samhradh'

This is one of my favourite traditional Irish songs. It dates back to the eighteenth century but is as fresh and colourful today as ever. It was traditionally sung on the first day of May to welcome the summer and it always reminds me of summer holidays as a child. Long, bright, school-free days, playing in the back field in Clondalkin and heading away on holidays.

I looked forward to the holidays so much and I think a lot of my pride and delight in our Celtic heritage is rooted in those times – not that I necessarily recognised it then!

Indeed, I had serious holiday envy when pals arrived home from their two-week sojourn in the sun with a souvenir doll in national costume or, my favourite, a Spanish doll with a mantilla, a ruffled flamenco dress and tiny castanets attached to her hands. This was the stuff of dreams, and it would remain so for many years until I was earning my own money and could afford to venture abroad on holidays.

We Kennedys holidayed with our cousins next-door, the Whites, and research began for the two mothers in January when they started to scour the small ads section in the newspaper. They had two criteria. First, the house must sleep all eleven of us and second, and most importantly, it had to be affordable.

I'm not exaggerating when I say that we holidayed once in a house where, at high tide, a river ran across the kitchen floor, separating the sink from the table. On another occasion, the leg of a bed went through the floor of a house we were renting, emerging like a stalactite in the sitting room ceiling! Money was tight and suffice to say our holiday rentals were basic.

Nevertheless, we all enjoyed ourselves enormously. The adults had grown up in Dublin city and they were as enthralled as their children by the places we visited, the more remote the better. And in order to be affordable, they were invariably remote.

They were also our introduction to life outside the city

and I believe the connection and respect that Deirdre and I have, along with our brothers and cousins, for the traditions and rural ways of Ireland stem from those times.

A holiday during the late sixties, to Geesala, Co. Mayo, was particularly memorable. The journey from Dublin to the Erris peninsula was epic. We had a picnic lunch at Lough Owel, outside Mullingar. Nowadays such a journey from Clondalkin would take no more than an hour and certainly would not merit a full picnic! And a full picnic it was. Cocktail sausages, served from a food flask, mountains of sandwiches, biscuits and oceans of tea.

The holiday featuring the leg of the bed coming through the ceiling was another delightful immersion in the rich heritage that is all around us in this country. Once again, it was a Kennedy/White adventure, this time in Spiddal, the entrance to the Galway Gaeltacht. We were there for *An Tine Chnáimh* on St John's Eve, and it was a highlight of that holiday. I didn't realise the significance of this ancient tradition at the time, but I still have a vivid memory of joining the local people around the fire down by the pier and being mesmerised by the hookers passing by on the sea and lowering their sails. I have witnessed this balletic display several times since while spending time with Deirdre on Inis Mór and every time I see it I'm brought back to that childhood holiday in Spiddal.

On St John's Eve, in traditions that go back to pagan midsummers, the boats are blessed for the year ahead, the fires are lit, and people gather around and some jump over the flames to bring good luck for the summer crops. Troublesome weeds are often thrown on the fire. People bring embers to their homes. Ashes are scattered on the fields. Cattle are presented to the dying embers. St John's wort and foxgloves are picked for their medicinal qualities.

Fire is a powerful element and continues to be significant in the Christian context, associated with the feast of St John. In fact, the pagan and Christian symbolism sit comfortably side by side. This poem was written by a Limerick poet in 1861. The bonfire on St John's Eve brought a flicker of light, a moment of joy to these people who, undoubtedly, had suffered so much in the aftermath of the Famine of the 1840s.

With festal fires the hills were lit!
Thine eve, St John, had come once more,
and for thy sake,
As though but yesterday thy crown were worn,
Amid their ruinous realm uncomforted
The Irish people triumphed.

– Aubrey Thomas de Vere

We all love summer holidays. They are times of rest and recuperation. They allow us to recharge our batteries, to be enthralled and uplifted by new places and people. I believe that when we holiday in Ireland, we sup at the well of tradition and our rich heritage and from that comes a sense of belonging, a pride of place and people. We are an ancient people. Our country has been inhabited for tens of thousands of years. We come from a race of hunter-gatherers, fishermen, farmers, resilient Celtic men and women who forged a living and developed a culture that has been passed to us through generations, making us the people we are.

That tribal sense was spotlighted during the Covid pandemic, when foreign holidays were suspended. Huge numbers of people who previously would have travelled abroad for their holidays were pleasantly surprised by how much they enjoyed their staycations. They spoke of the beautiful locations, the welcome, the sense of ease that made them feel at home.

The late comedian Hal Roach used to say: 'You know it's summer in Ireland when the rain gets warmer!' But the weather didn't interfere with our appreciation of our heritage in its various manifestations.

deirdre and mary

We are all close to the traditions that shape us, often unaware of how close until many years later. Our changing perspectives on the world, as time passes, offer us an opportunity to slow down and appreciate the gift of the passing seasons of our lives.

Though it is not always possible to visit places of heritage or great beauty, perhaps there is a chance to listen and see with the eyes and ears of the heart. Even a walk through a busy city can call us to notice the presence and sound of the birds as well as the hum of traffic, or to become aware of the new buds bursting with life on the familiar route to our home or place of work. Taking a contemplative walk in nature can restore a tired or troubled heart and bring a deeper awareness and intimacy.

Our journey continues as we look at the power of music, dance and pilgrimage, trusting in the words of the Persian poet Hafiz to guide our way ...

The Rose

How did the rose
Ever open its heart
And give the world
All its beauty?
It felt the encouragement of Light
Against its being,
Otherwise,
We all remain
Too frightened.

– Hafiz

music

deirdre

There is a tribe in Africa that sings to the unborn child in the womb during the pregnancy and as the child is being born. This is the 'soul song' of the newborn for the rest of their life. What a beautiful way of recognising the gift of each new child and the unique commitment and presence of the tribe and village. Each time their special song is sung the child is remembered. That strong link with their own sound and song connects deeply to their sense of belonging to a tribe and a story that stretches from generation to generation.

Music is a language that crosses many boundaries and, in an instant, can transport us to a different culture or landscape and can give us a sense of connection. In the Celtic world, the sounds of the natural world were listened to as music, the fifth element that connected to the spirits of the otherworld. The lilting breeze could conjure up a gentle blessing from the nearby spirits, or a lament in the keening at the death and loss of a loved one. Nature sounds were listened for intently, as in many other indigenous cultures worldwide.

Aboriginal song lines, which were walking routes that linked important sites and locations, are an incredible example of the power and nature of sound. The traveller on the road had to memorise and sing the song in order to follow the route to where they wanted to go. Imagine the possibility of a harmonious song to which we listened deeply to hear the sound of our own soul and the song of the very earth or area we inhabited?

In Ireland we are known for our music and song, much of which was passed on orally from generation to generation. Even the old tradition of lilting was a unique art of 'mouth music' in which traditional airs and tunes were sung, especially in the absence of musical instruments. *Sean nós* singing was a way of capturing the stories of love or loss and nights were spent listening to many verses of songs that captured the heart's journey of a people and its land.

Songs were sung to accompany every activity of daily life

from sowing seeds to milking cows to weaving wool and, at the end of a long working day, traditional lullabies in the Irish language were often sung by the women to soothe a child towards a calm and restful sleep.

That heartbeat connection between mother and child is perhaps part of the magic of the worldwide phenomenal response to *Riverdance*. The music, song and story tapped into the primal heartbeat of the world, offering a soul connection.

The healing power of music is perhaps one of the most wonderful gifts it offers and for me, it became a deep journey of listening and remembering that changed the course of my life significantly, opening up a song line that the heart heard and had to follow.

Growing up in Clondalkin, there was always a welcome in our house for a poem or a song. Our mam was a member of the local choir and Dad was more of a crooner with some old-time favourites like 'Frankie and Johnny' or 'One Alone'. There were great gatherings with our next-door cousins and relatives, where everyone was invited to do their party piece. Even if you were shy and didn't feel like performing, you at least knew that a great supper of sandwiches and treats was on the way. Our neighbour had a bull farm and having fed the egg yolks to his bulls, gave the remaining egg whites to our aunt and mam, who turned them into delicious high-peaked meringues dripping in cream and fresh fruit, which we tucked into as soon as all the songs were done and supper was served. It brought a real feeling of connection to our tribe and Mary has continued that tradition by being the one who loves to host a party with all kinds of party pieces being performed.

Following music as a profession was never really a considered option for us as the music business doesn't offer a permanent, pensionable career. We were given plenty of opportunities to avail of extracurricular classes, though, and our parents did all they could on a very tight budget to allow us to pursue these interests in the local community. Education and counselling became the path that unfolded for me, but I continued to notice a niggling call to music that just wouldn't go away!

Home Inside ...

There is a Song
Yet unsung, seeds of notes
Through darkened soil.
Lamentation,
Cry of the Earth,
River of tears its sound ...
Light of a new Melody
Mother sings ... rest awhile and listen
For a breath,
A Semi-breve ...
One Note,
Silence,
And a murmured chord
Towards Home ...

– Deirdre Ní Chinnéide

Sounds of tanks, tears and heart-rending stories became familiar during my work as a therapist in Bosnia and Kosovo, but the Aran Islands became my place of refuge following these trips, to rest in the silence and beauty of the natural world. It is there that I clearly heard a call to try to create music that would offer an alternative to the darkness of the haunting, discordant cacophony of conflict and war. Deciding to spend six months on the island became the catalyst for the writing of the music for *Celtic Passage*, an album that brings the listener on a journey of the heart through the depths of Celtic spirituality. For the next seven years, a deep inner journey unfolded and the music became a way of processing and singing through transitions and thresholds in my life.

Finally, in 2007, the album was launched in the USA as a musical experience, connecting to the power of the Celtic world while exploring themes of life and death, the earth and nature, the savagery of war, the redemption of love and ultimately the splendour of creation.

Celtic Passage calls us to remember, to return to the natural rhythms that link us to a deeper and more joyful experience of life, accompanied by the wisdom of our Celtic ancestors. Tracing our ancient story helps us to reconnect with and draw from the well of wisdom firmly rooted in our story, culture and heritage.

Music has brought me to many places, sharing the message of *Celtic Passage* through concerts, workshops and retreats. It is a wonderful experience to perform at Celtic festivals such as the Festival Interceltique in Lorient or the Milwaukee Irish Fest in the USA, gatherings of the very best of music from

Celtic countries worldwide. Just a note from an uileann pipe can resonate in the heart and make us proud to be Irish, with strong cultural roots in language, heritage and the soul.

In my retreat work, it is always quite moving to see how the music of *Celtic Passage* opens the heart to a remembering that often brings the listener to tears. My passion and purpose in composing and sharing music has always been to bring people to a place beyond words, where the heart resonates and responds to something being spiritually moved deep within them. When music offers comfort and hope, it becomes a healing balm that is worth its weight in gold.

My second album, *I Will Sing for You*, was due for release just before Covid got its grip on the world. All plans cancelled, like many others I found myself in lockdown waiting to see how this global crisis would unfold. It was hard to let go of my dream to release what I had called 'songs to soothe the soul', but miraculously another path emerged that had more of an impact in getting the music to places that would never have been reached in my original plan. I and a team of four wonderful friends decided to launch a project called 'Threshold for Hope', which would involve sharing music through an online evening of conversation and music videos, which offered solace and hope at a very difficult and challenging time.

The support and response were phenomenal and the event was seen by more than 6,000 people in thirty-two countries all over the world. It was moving to hear how the music had tapped right into the fragility and vulnerability that many people were experiencing during the Covid pandemic and it was a great privilege to offer something that travelled worldwide without leaving the safety and comfort of our own homes.

I love when music helps to heal a troubled heart and am always interested in helping people to release whatever might be blocking or holding them back from truly finding their voice and feeling a deeper connection to their own story and song.

This inner work may mean opening to many different seasons of the heart, but the ritual, story and connection through Celtic spirituality continually bring people to a sense of reconnection with a more peaceful place within. They find their way back to a 'soul home' they may have forgotten or never even knew existed. It is, I believe, an invitation to the depths of who we are and can be, constantly finding what it is that moves through the conflict of a divided heart to a more restful place of peace.

The final track of *Celtic Passage* is called '*Síocháin*', the Irish word for 'peace', which sings of a hope that in choosing the open hand of love and friendship we might journey to the gift and blessing of peace …

Where love and death are rooted
In the one divided tree
Meet me at a place
Where we both can freely be.

Where justice is a language
Not spoken in a land

May love of peace
Then guide us
To reach the open hand.

Síocháin, síocháin, síocháin, síocháin ...

May music continue to guide us through boundaries that separate us from ourselves, others and the very earth itself. In listening for new sounds, songs and melodies, may we hear the gentle lilting of the *Bealtaine* blessing, a full and bountiful mother as she sings ...

Let me wrap you in the Light.
Rest awhile ...
Assured of Memory
Circling Sound
To sing and sing again
An eternal Song of Love.

– Deirdre Ní Chinnéide

dance

deirdre

There is something quite unspoken in dance that is communicated through gesture, flow and movement. It's a tradition that has been core to our culture and heritage since ancient times. The Celts were sun worshippers who practised dance within a stone circle. It is said that they danced in a clockwise movement on happy occasions and anti-clockwise as an expression of mourning. There is no doubt that dancing in such a formation offers a feeling of belonging to a community and a way to express the many rituals and threshold times of the Celtic year.

We have spoken about the vibrant dance at *Bealtaine* around the maypole, and we can see the continuation of this style in set dancing, which is still being practised and enjoyed in villages and towns all over Ireland today. Many a night, dance lovers gather to spend the evening tapping their feet to the rhythm of the best of traditional music and twirling with their partners in intricate movements that have been passed down from generation to generation.

Long before dance halls were invented the people and the piper congregated at the village green or crossroads and young people especially were known to have danced, as the saying goes, 'till the cows came home!'

The Druids were known to use dance in ritual, honouring the oak tree or in adoration of the sun, and the tradition has endured through the centuries. The traditional *céilí* originally got its name from a gathering of folk in a neighbour's house and often the half door was removed on a night of such partying to be used as a floorboard for the *sean nós* dancer, a free style of movement that is quite different to the more formal group dances that are associated with the *céilí*.

Having spent time in the Gaeltacht on Irish language summer courses, both Mary and I were familiar with the shy excitement at seeing a fanciable suitor shuffle his way over to us, ready to pop the question, '*An ndéanfaidh tú damhsa liom?*' (Will you dance with me?). Many a budding romance was started after dancing the Siege of Ennis or the Walls of Limerick, leaving you on tenterhooks for the next night's *céilí* and the sight of the love of your Gaeltacht life! It didn't matter that your potential suitor had two left feet! At that stage you were just so happy not to be left waiting too long at the wall and to be chosen by potentially the man of your dreams, making learning Irish on a Gaeltacht course a hugely exciting experience!

We all might have benefitted from the dancing master who used to travel the length and breadth of the country in times gone by, teaching the steps the way they really should have been danced in the first place. On many occasions, the dancing master met with pupils who didn't know their right foot from their left and overcame this difficulty by tying some hay on one foot and grass on the other. To distinguish the steps he was trying to teach his students, he could often be heard shouting, 'Hay foot forward and grass foot back!' We would never have developed a love of culture and heritage if that was part of our *céilí* attire!

As soon as we learn to walk, dance follows and there is nothing more beautiful than seeing little ones move freely to music. How sad it is that as adults we can be self-conscious about dancing and perhaps we might benefit from following the quote that encourages us to 'dance like nobody's watching'.

Like music, the tradition of dance in different cultures expresses great grace and beauty and while style varies, there seems to be a common circular movement that is seen in many countries worldwide. Our Celtic tradition is no exception and the spiral dance is a common form that is increasingly popular and used for meditation and mindful movement.

There is a growing interest during Celtic spirituality retreats in using dance as a form of prayer and it is very affecting to see how body movement or gesture can express the deepest stirrings of the inner world. Meditation through dance is something that brings the body and breath into alignment, allowing the dancer to connect with emotions in an expressive way beyond words.

Our traditional slow airs can open the door to the healing of grief in particular and the body memory releases emotions that may never have been fully expressed in any other way. There is much research and evidence to show that dance can be healing as well as being an expressive form of art. I love to imagine what kind of dance we could create on a global level that would form a bond between people irrespective of race, colour, culture or creed. If our story were to be danced instead of spoken, it would be beautiful to feel the gentle movement of a dance that connects in friendship and peace.

The Sufi tradition of whirling dervishes is a great example of a community of dancers who pray their movement, with one arm extended in praise of the earth and the other in praise of the heavens. In response to the gospel in the Irish language we say the words *Seo é Briathar Dé*, which translate as 'This is the word of God' and also as 'This is the movement of God'. There is something quite mystical in the grace and fluidity of dance, and in Celtic times it would not have been unusual to dance to the moon, the sun, the sky and the stars.

In Ireland each year, an alternative *Dancing with the Stars* captures the hearts of the whole nation as a popular television programme on RTÉ. The magical transformation that happens, as newly formed dancers take to the floor, brightens and lifts the hearts of many, as it did our family when we followed the progress of our bright and shining sister and star. Proud as punch, we Kennedys watched Mary week after week, as she stepped gracefully into a new dance chapter of her already full and varied life!

maRy

The 'magical transformation' that Deirdre refers to with my participation in *Dancing with the Stars* took a long time and was physically demanding and mentally stressful. Despite those fairly major hurdles that had to be overcome, I feel nothing but joy, exhilaration and satisfaction when I think about those four months from November 2019 to March 2020. I'm aware those are the dark, cold months of *Samhain*, but dancing gave them the light, warmth, laughter and positivity of summer days. It surpassed my expectations and made me feel very happy to have accepted the invitation to strap on the ballroom and Latin dancing shoes: a magical experience from beginning to end.

Don't get me wrong. I was absolutely petrified from the moment I agreed to take part. I had been a fan of the show since it started on RTÉ but would never have imagined that I would take to the floor. I was not a dancer. Okay, I had gone to Irish dancing classes when I was in primary school, my mother deciding that they would help me to turn my toes out rather than in when I walked. She also believed Irish dancing would improve my posture. I was a bit 'round shouldered'. My two friends Mairead and Barbara Ann and I were escorted by our mothers on the 51 bus into North Great George's

Street every Friday night for our class at the Inis Ealga School of Irish Dancing, run by Mattie Maleady and his assistant Marie Duffy. We were not their star pupils! In fact, we three pals from Clondalkin spent more time in the back room practising the steps we were supposed to have learned from the previous week than we did in the main classroom dancing to the music. Something must have rubbed off on me, though, because I'm very glad to know Irish dancing steps and I like nothing better than dancing at a *céilí* or watching set dancers gliding around the floor to uplifting traditional music. I am in awe of the wonder that is *Riverdance* and feel very proud of its worldwide success. I never really got beyond first base with my classes, though. I still turn my toes in when I walk. And I'm still a bit round shouldered!

Fast forward half a century and I'm stepping way outside my comfort zone and agreeing to put my best foot forward. Only problem is I didn't have a best foot when it came to dancing! However, I knew I was off to a good start with John Nolan, my professional partner. Apart from the fact that he is a beautiful dancer, John is a lovely, down-to-earth, calm and gentle man. He is also an excellent and patient teacher who takes it, literally, step by step when embarking on a new routine. He is mature and wise beyond his years and he has a lot fewer years on the clock than I have. In fact, John is around the same age as my youngest daughter, Lucy. I am older than his mother! Despite the cavernous age gap, we got on brilliantly. I was in awe of his gifts of dancing and teaching and he was quite impressed by the fact that if he suggested any acrobatics as part of a dance, I was happy to give them a go!

The glitz and glamour of the Sunday evening show on RTÉ didn't come without a lot of effort, let me tell you. It was the culmination of a week's incredibly hard graft. John has a dance studio on the Long Mile Road in Dublin and we trained there seven hours a day, every day, Monday to Friday. The studio is called Xquisite but there was little exquisite about my efforts on a Monday at 8.00am as John was introducing me to that week's dance. I'm glad he didn't know about the dancing master of old who tied hay to one of the student's shoes and grass to the other! Mind you, it might have helped this doubly left-footed dancer!

I'd go home at three o'clock, feeling pretty dejected that I just couldn't get the hang of the foxtrot or the salsa or the Viennese waltz or the tango, or any dance for that matter. I didn't feel a whole lot better after Tuesday's efforts either and I have a memory of John saying every week: 'Don't worry. It's only Wednesday!' Then things seemed to fall into place. I'd remember where to put my feet and what the next sequence was. I'd stop overthinking it and give myself permission to just dance to the music. The exhilaration of dancing the routine from start to finish without making a mistake was the most satisfying feeling ever. I knew then that it was a case of improving and perfecting from that moment on and if Teacher was happy with the progress, we would take an hour's break and go for brunch on Friday. That didn't happen every Friday, if you know what I mean!

Saturday morning saw us all down in Ardmore Studios in Co. Wicklow, which were transformed into a mini-Hollywood set, comprising rehearsal space, studio floor, costume department, hair and make-up, catering and dressing rooms. ShinAwil, who make *Dancing with the Stars*, have the production honed to a fine art. We were really well looked-after. Good food, lots of rehearsal time, gorgeous costumes, fab hairstyles, beautiful make-up and I think I speak for all of my pals from the class of 2020 when I say that a real highlight was the spray tan that we got on Saturday evening after rehearsals. We'd arrive in Ardmore on Sunday morning glowing. There is nothing like a nice tan to make you feel good about yourself, and by the time the programme started, and we were lining up to dance, we needed all the extra little boosts we could get. The nerves were shocking. But when the music started and it was time to take to the floor, we gave it our all. And it was delightful to be part of this lovely experience.

When I look back on my adventure with *Dancing with the Stars*, I feel very grateful. I was given a wonderful gift when I took that step outside my comfort zone. I made new friends, most of them more than half my age. That didn't matter. We were all learning movement, feeling both nervous and exhilarated and gaining an appreciation of the incredible skill and creativity of the professional dancers.

There's a common bond that comes from dance. It is free-flowing, non-judgemental and, very importantly, a celebration of the body and what it can achieve through movement. As Deirdre said, there are no words necessary, yet there is great communication. Dance celebrates movement, fitness, physicality and fun. It teaches us to use our bodies in a confident and open way. This was a lesson worth learning for me. I grew up disliking my body. My generation of young Irish girls and women were taught to cover up and hide behind mountains of clothes. We were modest and self-conscious about our physicality. It's ironic that this attitude prevailed for so long when you consider that we come from a long line of strong Celtic women: saints, queens, landowners, pirates, from Brigid to Meadbh to Gobnait to Granuaile.

As I began my dancing journey, I was quite shy about wearing the really short and revealing costumes. The term 'mutton dressed as lamb' found its way into my vocabulary but thankfully didn't stay too long. By week two, I was dancing as if no one was watching.

Dance teaches us to celebrate our bodies and rejoice in physical health and fitness as we move in intricate sequences to beautiful music. I can't think of anything nicer. For this non-dancer, *Dancing with the Stars* was incredibly rewarding, life-affirming, exhilarating and so much fun.

Let us journey to the well of wonderful music and dance that has been handed down to us from generation to generation, is part of our celebration of our past and our present and brings joy, laughter, warmth and the light of summer into our lives. Let us channel our inner child and dance with gay abandon.

Soar into the Mystery
In taking flight,
Return to your place of landing
Like it was the first time,
But deeply knowing

Blessed as Pilgrims
On a journey
Home,

From stone
When rolled away ...
A Second chance

To Dance
Your Resurrection.

– Deirdre Ní Chinnéide

pilgrimage

Siúil, siúil, siúil a rún,
Siúil go sochair agus siúil go ciúin.

Walk, walk, walk, my love,
Walk gently and walk quietly.

– From '*Siúil, a Rúin*'

mary

There's a peaceful and gentle feel to the words of this
traditional song that belie its story of a woman bemoaning
the fact that her love is leaving. It's thought the song refers
to the Wild Geese, Irish soldiers who left Ireland to serve in
European armies, beginning with Patrick Sarsfield and his

men in 1691 after the Treaty of Limerick. Those were difficult circumstances to say the least, yet the quietly lyrical, almost whispered words lend themselves to a gentler interpretation. They always bring to mind for me the process of walking, of passing easily along the way. The reflective, thoughtful atmosphere they evoke reminds me of the many walks I have undertaken during long summer days. I always hum those lines when I'm embarking on a stroll in the countryside and they are the epitome of the mindful walking we all aspire to when we travel a holy way, a *camino*.

In Ireland we have a strong tradition of pilgrimage. Remember St Brigid and her journey from her home place of Faughart to Kildare, bestowing a holy well every place she stopped? Croagh Patrick is the most famous pilgrim path in Ireland. People have been climbing the mountain for thousands of years, honouring and following in the footsteps of St Patrick, who is said to have fasted on the summit for forty days. On Reek Sunday at the end of July, the paths are thronged with young and old, some barefoot, some carrying walking sticks, all availing of this journey to pay homage, to do penance, to seek intervention for a petition or to reflect on their lives. Many and varied are the reasons why people become pilgrims, but I believe that they are all afforded a feeling of self-awareness, of connection, of inner peace, similar to the whispering sounds of that lovely traditional air 'Siúil, a Rúin'.

I've climbed to the top of Croagh Patrick on a few occasions and every time I feel a great sense of belonging to a tribe. I'm very conscious of those who have walked this same path before me. I am of them. They are a spiritual, thoughtful, creative people who worked hard, who struggled, who suffered for their faith, who left Ireland and sought to bring compassion and support where they found want and sorrow. The religious significance of Croagh Patrick dates back to pagan times, when people gathered there to celebrate the beginning of the harvest season. Celtic spirituality and Christian spirituality sit comfortably side by side on this ancient mountain.

Summertime gives us a wonderful opportunity to explore our country and to embark on some pilgrim routes. That's not to say we can't follow the trails at other times of the year, but it's a lot more pleasant climbing mountains when the weather is mild. It suits me, certainly. I find it harder to be reflective, to think nice thoughts and contemplate mindfully when I'm battling the elements and feeling sorry for myself! Each to her own. There are no rules about following our inner path. I have had lovely experiences on pilgrimage alone with my thoughts, and at other times it has been nice to have company as we walk.

Giorraíonn beirt bóthar.

Two people shorten the road.

This Irish proverb has many layers. Certainly, when two people are walking together, the journey seems shorter. How often have you heard someone say: 'Gosh, are we there already!' We are a nation of talkers, intrinsically interested in finding a connection when we meet somebody for the first time. Historically, we are a nation of travellers, forced to emigrate during tough times, times of hunger during the Famine in the middle of the 1800s, and times of economic hardship in more recent years.

Everywhere we go in the world, we find our fellow country-men and women. The general perception is that the Irish are adaptable, hardworking, capable, creative, thoughtful. For such a small country, we certainly punch above our weight. We have reason to be thankful to our forebears for those qualities.

We derive from an ancient people. I was fascinated to learn from the RTÉ documentary *The Burren: Heart of Stone* that there are signs of human habitation in Ireland as far back as 30,000 years ago. That's a lot of heritage, with all its personality, character and belief systems, which has gone into the Irish make-up – from prehistoric times, including Neolithic, Copper, Bronze and Iron Ages, from Celtic pagan to Christian times.

As well as being an ancient people, we are a very diverse and resourceful one. No wonder, therefore, we don't go unnoticed on the world stage. Ireland has given over twenty presidents with Irish ancestry to the USA. In the developing world, where there is hardship and hunger, you will invariably find the Irish serving the needs of the people.

We have known hard times and that has given us an innate compassion for people who are less well-off. As a country, we care. The self-knowledge that is available to us as we take time out and walk thoughtfully is enormous.

There's something wholesome and satisfying about pilgrimage, physically, spiritually and emotionally, and the knowledge that people have been doing it for centuries in all sorts of different circumstances is very humbling. Humility is one of the cornerstones of pilgrimage. It's difficult to have notions of grandeur when you're struggling over fences, swatting horseflies or wasps or getting blisters on your feet. And that's when you're on a summer pilgrimage. Winter is a different ball game altogether.

The pilgrim's effort is always rewarded, though, by insight afforded into the lives of those who have gone before, by the opportunity to position ourselves in relation to those people, to step outside our daily routine and to gain self-awareness and a sense of what's important in life.

A lot of Irish people, myself and Deirdre included, have walked the Camino de Santiago, following the path of St James in Galicia in the north of Spain. We did the journey in early summer and you'll be glad to know that northern Spain has weather that mirrors our own at times. It lashed rain for five of the seven days that we walked the pilgrim paths. We were part of a group and I enjoyed the opportunity to walk with others and sometimes walk alone. There are many starting points for this *camino* and it wasn't until I signed up for it that I realised that one of them is in Dublin, at James Street church. That is where we got the first stamp on our pilgrim's passport. Later that summer, during a visit to Dingle, I saw the scallop shell decoration, synonymous with the Camino de Santiago, on the wall facing the Catholic church in the town and realised that it, too, had been a starting point for hundreds of years.

I was delighted that west Kerry, one of my favourite places in the world, has its role in such a meaningful pilgrimage. Delighted but not surprised. Dingle and its hinterland are steeped in Irish heritage and very close to my heart because that is where my love of our Irish language, literature and song began, at the age of sixteen, when I went there for the first time to learn Irish.

My Irish teacher in Coláiste Bríde was from Kerry and she organised for a small group of her fifth years to travel to Corca Dhuibhne and spend three weeks with a local family. We were studying *Peig* for the Leaving Cert and Mrs Redmond felt that it would be beneficial to spend time in Peig's area and soak up the way of life that she had experienced.

The family we stayed with were the Ó Conchurs, and they had a *siopa* directly opposite the church in Carraig, a tiny village between Ballyferriter and Feothanach. To say that the trip was an eye-opening experience doesn't do it justice. This was my first time away without my parents. It was an adventure. We were five very sensible sixteen-year-olds who were studying honours Irish and our parents trusted us to travel safely and to be well-behaved.

Their trust was rewarded because we were the epitome of good behaviour from the beginning to the end of the sojourn. Lack of opportunity may have played its part in our good behaviour, but I'll take the praise nonetheless! We read *Peig*, we chatted with the *bean a'tí* and her husband. We walked for hours every day. I can't speak for the others, but I was very definitely mesmerised by the people, the beautiful unspoiled landscape, the language, the culture. Corca Dhuibhne cast its spell on me. I loved sitting on the windowsill outside the *siopa*, listening to the *fear a'tí* chatting to his customers in the most beautiful Munster Irish, my favourite dialect to this day. It's soft, it's lyrical, it has a flow to it that is gentle and captivating.

I loved going into Dingle and walking the streets that Peig had walked when she was a *cailín aimsire,* working for a family in the town. The descriptions in her autobiography, of the housework she did, of serving behind the counter in the hardware shop and bar, of walking the streets of Dingle, came alive for me. The way I felt when I walked into Curran's shop is the equivalent, I would say, of an Elvis fan visiting Graceland for the first time.

I was amazed to find things were just as she had described them. I didn't realise it at the time, but that schoolgirl visit to Corca Dhuibhne in the summer of 1971 was a pilgrimage to a place that has remained central to my appreciation of our language and our culture. Every time I visit Dingle, I go into Curran's on Main Street and remember Peig, her story, her life with its joys and sorrows on the mainland and later on the Blasket Islands.

Peig was a strong woman of the land, a storyteller, a woman of faith, a mother who gave birth to eleven children, six of whom survived. She was a warrior. I thank her for the Irish womanhood that she embodied and which I absorbed willingly. I'm also thankful for the record she has left of life during the first half of the twentieth century.

When I later went on to teach Irish, it always gave me satisfaction to introduce my Dublin students to this strong woman, their forebear. Peig's story gave them a sense of their place as Irish women, informed their self-esteem and allowed them to appreciate their heritage.

I have Mrs Redmond to thank for that insight, at a young age, into our heritage. That trip to Corca Dhuibhne was the first of many for me. When I left school, I studied Irish in UCD and every academic year, I journeyed to the well of language, lore, song and dance in the Kerry Gaeltacht, delighted to be back in the heart of Peig country. It fed my soul to be walking the roads lined with fuchsia hedges, to be listening to the locals' melodic conversations, to be learning new ways of saying things *as Gaeilge*. I felt privileged to be part of such a rich and grounded culture. That pull to the replenishing cultural well of Corca Dhuibhne has continued throughout my adult life and it has been joined now by the pull to Inis Mór, where Deirdre lives and where reminders of our Celtic past abound.

Deirdre has a great knowledge of the Celtic monuments on the island, which she and I often visit. A couple of years after we undertook the pilgrimage on the Camino de Santiago, walking in the footsteps of St James, our group of friends gathered again to spend a few days on Inis Mór, in pilgrimage to our Celtic past. Deirdre was our guide and after that weekend everybody agreed our sense of belonging to a rich and important culture was beyond doubt.

The island is dotted with ruins of monastic settlements, holy wells and prehistoric forts, the largest of which is Dún Aonghasa. There is Celtic pagan and pre-Christian history and spirituality everywhere you walk on this sacred ground. These are the wellsprings from which we've come forth and we journey to their well to give meaning to our lives. They give us confidence in our sense of self and deep satisfaction as to our place on this earth.

The pandemic gave us an opportunity to walk more in our home surroundings – let's face it, there wasn't much else to do. But we embraced the opportunity to get outdoors, away from the home office or home schooling. We explored the nooks and crannies of our local areas and realised that a place takes on a different hue when you walk rather than drive through it.

I discovered a sturdy granite cross within my 2 km zone that had the date 1867 engraved on it. I learned afterwards that it was one of many erected as a precaution against cattle plague, which was decimating the herds of Co. Dublin, leading to a scarcity of milk and great distress a mere twenty years after the Great Hunger.

I had never seen this cross before or known that piece of local history and I've been living in the area for more than thirty years. When I walk that route now, I always remember the farmers of 1867 who struggled to keep their cattle healthy and their families fed in post-Famine Ireland. I thank them for their courage and their commitment to their livelihood. They are part of my tribe.

deirdre and mary

There was a sense of pilgrimage in those walks we all embarked on during the lockdowns. Our physical and mental health benefitted. They were certainly opportunities for reflection, for inner peace and self-awareness. We walked in our thousands during those challenging times and as we slowly emerge from restricted lifestyles, our wish is that we will continue to embrace the tranquillity of walking our land, bequeathed to us by our forebears, and will realise that we have deep wells of heritage, of resilience and of community from which to draw sustenance.

Having walked through the season of *Bealtaine*, we hope that you have travelled with a sense of how music and dance can celebrate and guide us along our pilgrim way. Perhaps Mark Twain's wisdom will settle gently in the light of an opening heart ...

> *Dance like nobody's watching*
> *Love like you've never been hurt.*
> *Sing like nobody's listening,*
> *Live like its heaven on earth.*

lughnasa

A Time to Reap

introduction

Mithid dom mo bhuíochas
A ghabháil libh a dhúile,
An comhar a dhíol libh.

It's time I made my gratitude
Known to you, you elements,
That I repaid your help.

– From 'Buíochas'/'Gratitude' le Máirtín Ó Direáin

deirdre

The season of *Lughnasa*, beginning on 1 August, halfway between the summer solstice and the autumn equinox, brings a time of celebration of the bountiful harvest of the earth. Our goddess in full maturity hums a melody of harmony, celebrating the release of her generous gifts. Ripened berries trail from many hedgerows, corn and potatoes are harvested with gratitude, while festivals and festivities mark the transition into this season of light. Lugh, whose name means 'light', was the chief god of the Tuatha De Danann – a supernatural race of the pre-Christian Celtic world – and his feast of *Lughnasa* brought endless opportunities for the community to reap the fruits of former labour and store sustenance for the dark winter months that lay ahead.

The closeness of their relationship with the earth as mother was reflected in the various blessings given and rituals performed at this time. It is lovely to see the link between each of the seasons we have explored in the natural relationship to the feminine and the growth from youthful bride to full and harmonious 'mother of the harvest'. It is said that sacred hills were climbed at *Lughnasa* and a cutting from the harvest corn was placed on the mountain as a gift to the great mother.

How interesting it is to draw on the well of wisdom of these indigenous communities and to see how some of these rituals are universal. In Peru, Mother Earth is given the name *Pacha Mama* and offerings are placed at the base of the mountain before a climber ever sets foot on it.

The connection between seasons is also honoured in the effigy of a woman seen at some harvest festivals here. People dance around her, pulling hair from her tresses, adorned with flowers and berries, and keep the grass and hair as bedding for Brigid during the season of *Imbolg* or spring.

It is a noisy time with the chatter and excitement of all that goes with the gathering at the local fair. Jams and jellies, vegetables and berries, stalls, vendors, pots, pans and the smell of animals herded and waiting for a new home. People gathered together in gratitude for the abundance and blessings of this rich and bountiful time. As with other seasons, bonfires were lit, dances were danced and the chance of losing or gaining a partner was part of this time of flirtation and gaiety!

Like all other threshold times, the spirit of the *Sí*, or faery folk, was never far away and the leprechaun himself, also known as *Lugh Chorpán* or 'little Lugh', was often heard tapping away in the forest with a little twinkle in his eye.

The earth takes a well-earned breather to enjoy the success of work that was done in the earlier seasons when tiny seeds were carefully planted in the tilled and furrowed land. We take a trip now with Mary to the Ploughing Championships, one of the most popular examples of a link to our ancestors and the tradition of reaping and working closely with those who still honour and celebrate the deep connection they nurture with the very ground that is and has always been a place we should and could call Home.

mary

Every season has its joy and there's a completeness about *Lughnasa*, with its feeling of satisfaction at a job well done. This is the time to reap the rewards of the physical work of sowing in the earlier parts of the year when *Samhain* gave way to *Imbolg* and the soil warmed up enough to be turned and planted. *Bealtaine* was a time to nurture those plants and now that *Lughnasa* has arrived, it's time to harvest.

In Ireland, the harvest is wonderfully celebrated with festivals, the largest of which is, of course, the National Ploughing Championships. The tradition of ploughing goes back a long way in Ireland. Around 3000 BC, Neolithic farmers used polished stone axes to fashion cultivation patches. The most primitive type of plough, the ard, probably came into Ireland in the later phases of the Bronze Age, around 700 BC. Since then, the plough has evolved and the job is done by tractors of all shapes and sizes with sophisticated attachments.

But the skill of a master ploughman, controlling a horse-drawn plough, opening the furrow and producing a lovely undulating pattern in a straight line, remains something to behold. It's not easy, believe me. I've tried it and 'undulating', 'straight' and 'furrow' are not words anyone would use to describe my efforts! Not surprising, really. I am fully aware of the amount of time it takes to master this amazing skill, because for about fifteen years I was fortunate to present *Nationwide* from the National Ploughing Championships.

I was hooked straight away. I loved everything about the event from the ploughing matches to the trade exhibitions to the fashion shows, the music and dancing and not forgetting the lines of shiny new machinery, where you'd be dwarfed by the height and the girth of these arresting examples of engineering.

The event has increased in popularity every year since it was first held in 1931 in Athy, Co. Kildare. It's a celebration of rural Ireland and a fitting tribute to our Celtic heritage. It's generally agreed that the Celts introduced horses and cattle to Ireland and they used them to plough the land for planting seeds and for grazing.

And so it continues. Every September, all roads in rural Ireland lead to 'the Ploughing'. The year's work is done and now is the opportunity to gather, meet old friends, make new ones, dance, sing, celebrate farming. It is, quite simply, a great day out. There's fun and laughter, learning and teaching and I have yet to meet somebody who hasn't enjoyed their day at the Ploughing.

The organisation of this major event is a credit to Anna May McHugh, who has been at the heart of the championships for more than six decades. She began as a secretary at the age of seventeen and has been managing director for more than forty years. Anna May's energy and professionalism belie her eighty-eight years. She and her daughter Anna Marie head up a dynamic team of 'can-do' people. Anna May is a strong Irish woman, a credit to her gender. A huge army of volunteers works closely with her to ensure the success of this celebration of our rural heritage at this important time of harvest. The sense of community and neighbourliness is tangible and something to be cherished.

The National Ploughing Championships are an integral part of the social and economic calendar in rural Ireland and there was a huge gap in that calendar during the pandemic. I have no doubt, however, that in time the hardworking organisers and volunteers will rally to the Ploughing, buoyed by their journey to the well of interconnection, community and pride of place.

The Ploughing Championships are held in different venues around the country, where farmers are only too happy to host this important event. In 2019, that venue was Ballintrane, Fenagh in Co. Carlow, a part of the country that is very dear to Deirdre and myself. Our maternal grandmother, Annie Dowdall, née Hogan, grew up there before she moved to Dublin to marry and rear her family of seven just off the North Circular Road.

I know Annie always missed her home place and spoke with affection of landmarks such as the Fighting Cocks pub and the church in Newtown, in the grounds of which her family members are buried. I also know that every Thursday morning, when cattle were driven along the end of her avenue on their way to the cattle markets in Smithfield, she made her way down to watch them pass, to listen to them and to inhale their smell. This was a highlight of her week and reminded her of her roots in rural Co. Carlow. It was also something her grandchildren enjoyed when we visited her on a Thursday. Deirdre and I, along with our brothers and cousins, would race down to the end of Ellesmere Avenue to watch the parade of cattle along the North Circular Road. We loved hearing the lowing of the cows, the sound of their hooves, the sweet smell on the air as they passed by. And I know I speak for us all when I say the highlight of our summer was the annual trip to Granny's home place in Carlow.

On the appointed Sunday, our parents would pile the four of us into the back of our Ford Anglia and head out the Naas Road in the direction of Carlow. The routine was the same next door with Auntie Eilish and Uncle Tom, except their three boys were piled into the back of their Volkswagen Beetle. The back seats of both cars were filled with moaning about being 'squashed' but all whinging stopped when we arrived at the farm of Granny's good friend Kate Esmonde and her brother Mick at the Fighting Cocks.

We poured out of the cars and enjoyed a day of freedom, adventure and great food. We climbed haystacks, herded (chased) sheep, fed pigs and collected eggs. I even brought a hen for a walk around the yard once – on a lead! We feasted on bacon and cabbage and delicious floury potatoes, followed by apple tart and fruit cake.

When we left for Dublin, we were laden down with vegetables, cakes and jams. Kate, Mick and their nephew Seán, who farmed with them, always made us feel very welcome. I'd say, though, it took them a week to recover from the visit of seven exuberant youngsters for whom the day on the farm was the equivalent of a trip to Disneyland nowadays. Our life was city-centred but our country heritage satisfied us greatly, even though we were two generations removed from life on the land.

Mick and Kate have long since left this earth but Seán still farms to this day. It was a very proud moment for him and his neighbours when their farms were chosen to host the 2019 National Ploughing Championships. Because of my connection with Seán's farm, we decided to visit him for *Nationwide* and take a trip down memory lane before the Ploughing. It was so lovely to be in the old farmhouse again, to go to the henhouse, to look around the yard. And the fact that Uncle Tom was a dab hand with the Super 8 cinecamera when we were young meant there was video evidence of our adventures on the farm as children, including me walking the hen around the yard! Seán and I sat in his kitchen and watched the old footage, remembering those happy times.

The visit to Seán's farm was undoubtedly a journey to the well of connection to the past and hope for the future. The seeds had been sown more than a hundred years ago when Annie Hogan was born in Newtown and became friendly with Kate Esmonde from the Fighting Cocks. The seeds were nurtured by Annie's daughters, Mam and Auntie Eilish, bringing their children on summer visits to the farm. Now it was time to harvest the goodness of those family ties, the simple pleasures, the wholesome relationships. *Lughnasa* was complete that day when Seán and I remembered with affection our departed loved ones.

deirdre

Linking in with the spirit of our ancestors makes us feel less alone. We connect to our story in a deeper way, bringing with us both the shadow and the light of what has gone before. In the Celtic tradition, this link with the spirits of those who had passed to *Slí na Fírinne*, or 'the way of truth', was encouraged and recognised as an important connection to the wisdom and experience of those who had walked and lived on the land before us. Autumn colours create great splendour at *Lughnasa*, as bright red, orange, yellow and almost gold leaves remind us of the changing tides of this time in the seasons of our own lives. We witness the elegance of the tree as it yields to an invitation in autumn to let go gracefully of its leaves, trusting that in due course new buds and shoots will herald the arrival of a new season and possibility for growth.

The land of the *Sí* of Celtic mythology could be journeyed to at will by the Druid or Shaman at threshold times such as this, returning with insight into the problems and challenges of everyday life. I wonder what wisdom the Druid would bring from the land of the *Sí* for our world today, especially in the time of Covid-19? Would he or she beat their drum loudly until we heard the rhythm of the earth, struggling to return to the oft-mentioned 'new normal' and adjust to what is being asked of us?

'*Sí Gaoithe*' or 'Spirit Breeze' is a song I wrote and included in the album *Celtic Passage*. It speaks of the breeze from the spirit world bringing a message to us from the ancestors.

> Arise a chroí
> Is éist leis an ngaoith
> Fad a mhairimid beo
> Fad a mhairimid beo.

Open your heart so that
you may listen to the sound
of spirit breeze

Bhur gceol scaoiligí
In eineacht leis an ngaoith
Fad a mhairimid beo
Fad a mhairimid beo

Release the sound of your
spirit with the light of spirit breeze

Do Anam do ghlór
Is na haingeal go leor
Ag casadh leat in éineacht leis an Rí
Ag casadh leat in éineacht leis an Rí

May your soul sing
with the angels of God

Do Anam do ghlór
Do Anam do ghlór

Listen till you see
All that you can be

Let the Wind bestow
The grace to know
For the path was clearly shown

The path was clearly shown
If you listen you will see
All that you can be
Soul sings peacefully
Soul sings peacefully.

How might we harvest the wealth of *Lughnasa* as we reflect more deeply on our story and the essence of this time of change? In many ways this season might find us reminiscing about earlier times of youth and vitality as we settle into the mid-life of our soul's journey. Imagine the richness in finding our own personal way of ritualising the letting go or gathering of this significant time. Inis Mór lends itself to such opportunities and in another chapter, I will share the fruits of the participants' experience when they come to the island for a retreat in Celtic spirituality.

There is a lovely story that a woman on the island told me of how she honours these later years in her life in a very natural and wholesome way. Every evening, in her bungalow in the west of the island, a little nightlight shines through the glass of her hall porch door. She explained that she lights this candle to offer peace to her global family of humans, plants and animals and from her doorway sends her intention of peace and light far and wide.

On her significant birthday she began her day with a silent prayer of gratitude, lighting the candle in what she described as her own chapel, right in the heart of her home. She later walked to the local well and did the rounds seven times, giving thanks for each of the seven decades of her life. She is a woman who walks gently on the earth, aware that each season offers a teaching and nourishment that brings her more deeply into the blessings and gifts of the path she has travelled.

Lughnasa offers us time to pause, reflect and reconnect with whatever might be holding us from an opportunity to drink and be nourished from the well. Surrounded by the presence, wisdom and elegance of nature, we can 'listen till we see, all that we can be ... for the soul sings peacefully ... soul sings peacefully'.

Let us take this time to settle and lean into the gifts of this full and fruit-filled time – opening the heart, listening deeply and learning to let go and release ...

Release

Now is the season to know
That everything you do is sacred.
This waiting time,
This listening time
Of Winter, Summer
Spring and Autumn ...

In the letting go
Through silence, light and love,
Let Autumn leaves return to seed.
For in their rhythm, rhyme and time,
They too can stretch
And make their way through darkened soil.
In peeping towards

A shard of welcome light ...
Release their sound
And giggle with delight.

– Deirdre Ní Chinnéide

Retirement

Mary

At *Lughnasa*, as we prepare to slow down as *Samhain* approaches once again, we have a chance to look inward and begin to become more still. Perhaps retirement can be conceived in this way.

My own retirement, at the age of sixty-five, was a requirement of my job in public service broadcasting. I loved the job, travelling around the country, meeting people with stories to tell and giving them a platform on national television. There was always a warm welcome for the *Nationwide* crew when we visited a city, town or village. It was interesting to meet new people and hear about their enterprise, their struggles, their relationships, their home place. I didn't want it to end.

Nevertheless, retirement knocked on my door, despite my unwillingness to embrace it. My colleagues at RTÉ laid on a fabulous going-away party with delicious food, wonderful video greetings and very kind speeches from management. Marty Whelan was the MC and I was very grateful for all the good wishes and support. It was a wonderful evening with family, friends and colleagues.

My first grandchild, Paddy, was eight months old at the time. He was allowed stay up late that night so he came along, in a new party outfit, and quite simply he stole the show! I have great photos of the night and lovely memories, but I was sad and lonely leaving *Nationwide* behind. I was no longer an employee of RTÉ. My ID card would no longer raise the barrier when I drove onto the campus or open the door to the studio. I was now officially retired and it did not feel good. Not yet.

Like many facing retirement, I grappled with feeling out of the loop, cast aside to be part of a different tribe of people who used to be important but were less so now, who used to have busy lives but did not have them now. I felt these demeaning and negative emotions, despite the fact that I knew I still had the possibility to work part time, and I went almost immediately into *Dancing with the Stars*.

The logic of the Celtic cycle of the seasons and of life was definitely not part of my thinking as I entered retirement. I feel very differently now, and for this, I'm grateful.

I am lucky to have always had good health and lots of energy. Just as well because there were very demanding periods during my working life: early starts, late finishes, day on day.

None of that bothered me. I loved challenges, opportunities, adventures. I was always on the go. There is a school of thought that considers busyness to be a badge of honour, an indication of importance, achievement, status. I know now that it is not. One's sense of self has to emerge from within. I really could not envisage what life would be like without those absolutely hectic schedules. Do you know what I've discovered? Life is good without them.

While we are part of the workforce, so many of us are defined by the job that we do. The development of technology and the sophistication of business practices during the later part of the twentieth century and since has increased productivity and resulted in the emergence of a vicious circle of more productivity leading to more demands.

Producing more invariably necessitates longer working hours. There has been an expectation that workers would stay on late to finish a job, that the rewards would be enjoyed further along the career path. A culture developed of judging ambitious and hardworking people by their willingness to work all the hours that God sent. The lines between work life and personal life became more blurred.

We've all witnessed or been part of the long queues of cars snaking into the cities from commuter towns from silly o'clock in the morning. Driving those cars would be workers who had perhaps woken sleeping babies and young children to leave them to childminders before sunrise, in order to make it into work on time.

In the evenings, the same traffic jams would fill the routes out of the towns and cities and many workers would be lucky to get home in time to kiss their children goodnight. Hand on heart, I don't think anybody could describe that as a wholesome way of life.

For all the suffering and sacrifice that the pandemic brought with it, as we look back on those days, we do well to acknowledge another change that came about at that time, namely, a realisation that there's more to life than work and material acquisition. Perhaps what might be seen as a new world order is gradually and tentatively emerging.

Around the world, people have been pushed to journey to their different wells for sustenance and direction. Forced to stay at home, they have looked more deeply into their own cultures, to find riches at hand.

In Ireland we fall back on our strong tradition of connection to the earth and to other people. We sow, we nurture and we harvest, literally and metaphorically, and every season has its place and value in bringing meaning and a sense of wellbeing to our lives.

I am in the *Lughnasa* of my life, at a stage where I now reap what I have sown. I can enjoy the fruits of my labours through the years. Retirement, followed closely by the pandemic, forced me to relinquish parts of my life that I valued. There followed a period of adjustment, of coming to terms with a new way of being, a new way of relating, a new way of enjoying life and living, and it all revolves around people and relationships. It took a while for me to recalibrate my body clock, but I did and now I'm savouring the benefits.

There is no hope of joy except in human relations.

This is true! I have been known to quote that line from *Le Petit Prince*, by Antoine de Sainte-Exupéry, on many occasions. It's simple, direct and it makes so much sense. It's a lesson that was brought home to us by the pandemic when we were prevented from hugging those whom we love. Let it be a lesson that we take with us into 'the new normal'. Let us value the slower pace of life that allows more time for loved ones and for leisure. Let us embrace the different seasons and seek balance and a slower pace in our lives.

Is glas iad na cnoic i bhfad uainn.

This Irish *seanfhocal* corresponds to the English maxim 'the faraway hills are always green'. May we journey to the well of contentment, of sufficiency, and realise that in the best tradition of *Lughnasa*, an abundant harvest brings enough and enough is plenty.

a time
for reflection

deirdre

*The Breath of God blows on the sails of the spirit
and gives movement to the boat of the heart.*

– Francis de Sales

Taking the boat from the mainland to Inis Mór starts a
journey with a difference. Leaving the busyness of life and
the constant hum of traffic, with the sounds of the waves
lapping on the side of the boat in harmony with the hum

of the engine, you are carried through the ocean feeling that you are on the way to a special experience. Out on the horizon, as land appears, there is a sense of excitement and mystery as you journey towards time out from the activities, responsibilities and concerns of everyday life.

To come to the island on retreat, you arrive not as a tourist but as a pilgrim who commits to spending the next few days soaking in the silence and gift that such a place has to offer. You gather with others in a unique landscape and, through immersion in the essence of Celtic spirituality, you begin your *turas an chroí* or journey of the heart.

The core of Celtic spirituality lies in the acknowledgment of the sacred in all things. There is a divine presence in all of nature and an invitation to experience the power of a deeper listening in journeying to the well of our personal and collective wisdom.

The word 'Celtic' has often been misrepresented as New Age but is in truth both ancient and new, in offering us a link to an ancient spirituality that can guide and support us in our everyday lives. We have already taken a journey through the seasons of the Celtic year, learning of the rituals and blessings that were of great importance to our ancestors with their strong connection to and reliance on the earth. In *turas an chroí*, we listen to our own inner nature, moving in the direction of a life of connection, balance and acceptance of the changing seasons of our lives.

Our various programmes offer a contemplative experience using music, art, poetry, prayer and movement with an invitation to spend time listening in the beautiful setting and landscape of the island of saints and scholars. There can be a period of readjustment as pilgrims adapt to their new surroundings. But following a good night's sleep and hearty nourishment in the fine guesthouses that provide accommodation, the soul begins to settle and feel cradled in the arms of the island, ready to be renewed and refreshed by its journey to the inner and outer well.

One of my favourite passages in scripture is the story of the woman from Samaria, healed by an encounter with Jesus as she drinks water from the well that promises to quench her eternal longing and thirst. There is an eternal longing at the heart of our human journey, and having time to stop and reflect on troubles and transitions in our lives can be a great source of healing for ourselves and others. I am grateful for my training as a psychotherapist and a spiritual director, which allows me the privilege of working with and sharing the healing gifts that retreats on the island have to offer.

Visits and ritual at the sacred sites evoke an atmosphere that was blessed by those who have gone before us. Pilgrims speak of a sense of presence they feel by having time to listen, notice and walk the boreens, embraced by the silence and beauty of nature. Totally resting the heart and soul helps to restore a weary pilgrim and send them happily on their way, following their time in the mystical landscape of Inis Mór.

Personally, I have always found retreats to be an important part of my own spiritual practice and growth and every year would travel to monasteries or retreat centres in Ireland or abroad.

My work now takes me to some of these same centres as a facilitator and I feel so grateful to share the Celtic Christian story with pilgrims in the USA, Australia and many parts of Ireland. The work is intense but brings with it the gift of creating programmes and workshops of music, scripture, poetry and prayer in a dynamic and creative way. I always come away from these retreats feeling the sacredness of connecting to people at a soul level, enriched by the journey we share together, honouring and deepening the call and exploration of the Divine.

The old patriarchal system of the Church cannot serve our full needs. Excluding the grace and beauty of the feminine leaves many searching for a spirituality that offers an inclusive community for all. The deep connection of Celtic spirituality to the earth as mother brings a strong message of our need to honour and respect her and is in line with the message of *Laudato Sí*, written by Pope Francis in recent years. We are beginning to see that change is inevitable and, rather than needing to be feared, it provides us with great possibilities for renewal and growth.

The marriage that is the Celtic Christian story is of great relevance to the islands and other sacred sites in Ireland, returning to a remembering of the roots of our tradition and faith. Perhaps these times of great change bring with them an opportunity to open the heart to a sense of belonging, community and hope for a way forward, especially during challenging times.

'*Oscail mo chroí*', 'open my heart', became my own prayer chant for many years and a pathway that forged my connection to Celtic spirituality and how it can support us in our daily lives.

In 2007, following the launch of my album *Celtic Passage*,

I decided to consider doing retreat work on the Aran Islands. Given an acceptance that the demands of everyday life can often leave us feeling dissatisfied, burnt-out or a bit lost, this musical journey travels from a divided heart to a homecoming to a more settled place within ourselves. While sharing the music through concerts was wonderful, I felt that if people came to the island on retreat, they could have their own personal experience of *Celtic Passage* and see how the island can support and nourish the soul's journey with a strong connection to the roots of our collective spirituality of great depth and richness.

Those who responded to the invitation came from far and wide. I and a team of other therapists enjoyed the beauty of the work, witnessing huge transformation in those who came on retreat. The work developed over many years and in 2019 I took a leap of faith and decided to build a permanent retreat space by converting an outdoor storehouse on the grounds of my house in Kilmurvey. With part-funding from some state organisations and religious orders I was able to 'turn the sod' and set the project in motion with excitement and anticipation.

My house looks directly on to Dún Aonghasa, a prehistoric fort, one of many that is visited by thousands of people who come to the island every year. It is a very powerful place perched high on the cliffs and I love to have these amazing ancestors as neighbours, even if they can't always deliver when you run out of a drop of milk!

We always incorporate a visit to the Dún as part of our retreat work and people are often overwhelmed by the power and presence that they feel there. John O'Donohue, the famous philosopher and writer, would also bring groups to the Dún, getting them to lean over the edge of the cliff and reflect on their own mortality! There is no doubt that as you walk up the hill towards the fort you can mindfully reflect on threshold times in your life and the gifts and challenges that may have accompanied you along the way.

In Celtic mythology, Aonghus was the God of Love, so the new retreat centre was named Slí Aonghusa, 'the way of love'. There is something powerfully profound about following the way of love and, irrespective of faith, tradition, colour or creed, love can go a long way to unite us in a spirit of respect, kindness and friendship with each other.

As with any building project, there were sleepless nights and anxious concerns, but it felt like the spirits were always standing nearby with help and support to bring this project to completion. The builders were probably a little surprised to find me placing numerous miraculous medals in the foundation before the cement was laid and many friends prayed a special intention for those who would come to use the place in the days that lay ahead.

The first group that arrived on retreat were women from Ballymun in Dublin city. Led by Lillian O'Brien, they left their homes at the crack of dawn to journey to the island. Many of them were moved to tears as they felt a warm and restful presence crossing the threshold of Slí Aonghusa for the first time and then enjoying the customary tea and scones.

For me, the space was truly blessed with the sacredness of their stories during their retreat and the grace they brought in the honest sharing of every season and challenge of their lives. The plan to house other groups at the centre was badly affected by the arrival of Covid and the space lay idle with the exception of my using it during the various lockdowns and pandemic restrictions. It was strange to have built a beautiful place in good faith and with great intention and to now not have any idea of how the next step might be taken.

As the whole world had been stopped in its tracks, there was nothing to do but to sit and wait. It gave me plenty of time to reflect on a vision of the kind of groups that might benefit from a retreat at Slí Aonghusa. The list is endless, but my heart really hopes that in the future, vulnerable groups who might not get the chance to visit such a space might come and feel the 'arms of the universe' holding them with care and kindness. Following the global experience of the Covid pandemic, I feel that there will be a need to gather in such spaces, to have conversations about the journey we have all made and to heal as we return to a changed reality and world.

'Come back to me with all your heart and I will give you rest' is a line from scripture that nourishes and heals the pilgrim who chooses to walk this way. We all need time to pause and listen so that we can take care of ourselves by making an inner journey and having the courage to accept ourselves exactly as we are. Life is hard at times and there is nothing more rewarding than spending time with others in a beautiful space, feeling supported and nourished by fellow companions. A friendship and deep bond develops between pilgrims on retreat as they share the reality of how they are in the presence of each other.

Pilgrims release burdens they have been carrying for a long time and it is as if a stone is rolled away from a formerly troubled heart. In gratitude to each other and to the ancestors, healing calls the heart to its place of rest and home ...

> A *Stone of earth*
> *Through dust its birth*
> *As starlight circles this dome.*
> *Let all who have witnessed and all yet to see ...*
> *That the ancestors' call is to home.*

– From *Celtic Passage*

There is a lovely tradition of the *anam cara* or soul friend in Celtic spirituality. Your *anam cara* is someone with whom you can really be yourself, sharing the highs and lows of your everyday life, knowing you will be listened to with care. It is nice to think of the soul friends that have supported us through life.

It is said that there is no such thing as strangers, just friends that we have yet to meet!

Celtic spirituality calls forth the very best in us, honouring that we are made in the image and likeness of the Divine. Who knows what that means for any of us? There is a reality, however, in that we all share the same planet, walking a journey that leads to the same threshold transition in time.

Perhaps there is great wisdom in the Celtic gift of hospitality to guide us along our way ...

You will have left your mark on the world
When each new stranger
Becomes a possibility
For friendship
And for love
And then you smile …

– Deirdre Ní Chinnéide

final steps

deirdre

For myself and Mary, the journey to the well represented in these pages began as sisters reminiscing about our younger days in Clondalkin, living near to St Brigid's well at the bottom of our road. Many seasons have been travelled by us both and I think it is safe to say that each time we return and pass by our house, number 31, memories are evoked with poignant fondness of a childhood spent there many years ago.

Over the course of our life experiences, we have both learned the truth of 'a season for everything' and though there have been many challenges and celebrations along the way, there is always a feeling that life moves through all experiences and it is in sharing these that we create community and a sense of connection with others.

There is always light around the corner in the natural movement from one season to the next. The seeds that are planted wait in the darkness of *Samhain*, in full trust that spring brings an opening of gentle hope, as new life emerges following the depths of winter.

Brigid, our spirit guide, offers an image of creativity, fertility, protection and possibility, growing into blossom in *Bealtaine* and fully matured by *Lughnasa*. Representing the Divine Feminine, she invites us to remember the roots of our spirit and connection with all living things.

Celtic spirituality found its way to our hearts especially during times we have spent on the Aran Islands and at other sacred sites in Ireland. Our journey to the well of this book made us delve deeper into our own thoughts, feelings and experiences, drawing on the waters that often nourished and refreshed our weak and weary souls. It has been good to remember that as we come near the end of our *camino*, there is so much that we are grateful for and that has blessed us along the way.

mary

We sisters, like so many other people, have a lot to be thankful for. Our lives are very different, one from the other, with one of us living on a western isle, steeped in Irish culture and heritage, and the other living in a capital city, which has become increasingly busy and cosmopolitan. We both share, however, a belief that family, community and relationships in general are central to our wellbeing. We also realise, as Deirdre said, that life travels through all experiences, some happy, some sad.

> Ní thuigeann an sách an seang.
>
> *The well fed do not understand the emaciated.*
>
> – Traditional Irish saying

Irish *seanfhocals* have a way of hitting the nail on the head. They offer pearls of wisdom and insight. It is only by living through difficult times that we understand the struggles of others. Our journey to the well has taken us to better times, ultimately, but I believe it is important to acknowledge those dark moments, to accept the difficult times that we all lived through. The pandemic certainly was a threshold time for people in Ireland and all around the world, when life as we knew it stopped and uncertainty entered our lives.

Our journey in these pages became a way of navigating this uncertain time, and it was satisfying to travel through our ancient Celtic heritage and to recognise its central position in bringing meaning into our lives. Deirdre and I hope that this journey through the Celtic year has given context and clarity to the challenges we all faced, our resilience in dealing with difficulty, followed by the emergence of green shoots in *Imbolg* and the lighter brighter seasons, which saw our confidence return slowly, restoring our sense of place in the world.

Our divine feminine mentor, Brigid, led the way for us to embrace new life and light, renewed possibility, fertility and harvest. Her thread runs back to our earliest days when our parents married and bought a house in Clondalkin, and their families thought they were moving to the sticks! They had both grown up in the city, a mere thirty-minute walk from O'Connell Street, and here they were setting up home in a tiny village in west Dublin, where the few streets and housing estates quickly gave way to fields and farmland and which didn't have a regular bus service at the time. Their decision was questioned by families and friends who were sure they would be lonely being so far away; but they settled swiftly, became active members of the community and lived in the house they bought in 1953 and in which they reared their family, until, in turn, each of them was taken to the Church of the Immaculate Conception in the village for their requiem mass.

Our mother and father embodied so many of the characteristics of our Celtic ancestry. They volunteered for every initiative that went towards building the community of Clondalkin into what it is today. Daddy was a founder member of Clondalkin Credit Union, Tidy Towns, Muintir na Tíre and the Clondalkin Dramatic Society. Mammy was part of the ICA, the church choir, the country markets – I told you Clondalkin was very rural back in the fifties!

They embraced our Irish culture and loved a good sing song at family gatherings. They were conscientious providers for their family and they had a deep faith. I wonder what they would have made of Deirdre and me exploring together our

Celtic past and its spiritual dimensions? I think they would be pleased that Brigid's legacy facilitated our journey to an inner well of thought, honest emotion and solidarity. As pioneers of community in their adopted village, I know they would value the fact that the heartfelt wish of their daughters – embarking on this book with a view to navigating through a time of loss, fear and uncertainty to a time of hope and renewed optimism – was to bring our readers along that path with us to a place of wellbeing and contentment.

Their memory lives on in their daughters' desire to connect with the values they gave us and to share them with people along life's journey.

deirdre and mary

As we meet this journey's end, we hope that you feel nourished and refreshed.

Standing at the edge of a new threshold can bring a feeling of anticipation, leaving what is familiar behind.

Yet something often beckons us to trust 'this crossing place', opening to new roads that lie ahead.

Is there something you can gather from this journey to the well so that the seasons of the Celtic year might help you become familiar with your own heart's journey and new thresholds that may emerge?

Perhaps such a time of turmoil that was heralded by the pandemic also offers an invitation to return to the wisdom of our ancestors. They walked in tune with the natural rhythm of the earth, listening deeply for signs and sounds that echoed in the wisdom of a deeper relationship with all living things. Imagine a world where we felt truly part of this community, sheltering under the cloak of Brigid, humming a new melody of kindness, care and generosity to ourselves, each other and the very earth itself. Singing in harmony, we open to a new dawn, new tides making their way to our shore with blessings of love, life and gratitude.

We thank you for having walked with us from Brigid's Road through the seasons of the Celtic year. May the path ahead be blessed with new seeds of hope that gently germinate in the landscape of your precious heart.

In and through a mother we came ...

Gently cradled of the earth.
Walk hand in hand.
Let light announce
A birthing of the new.

Embraced by Love
In who we are and can be ...

Oscail agus éist le do chroí
(open and listen to the heart)

– Deirdre Ní Chinnéide

permissions

Image on p.X used with the permission of the Lyons' Family

Danu Images (danuimages.com): 46, 58

iStock: vi/Anna Winterstein; xvi-1/Chris Hepburn; 2/Nicole Silvestri; 16/
LCBallard; 26/LCBallard; 44–45/Albert Mi; 70/Borisb17; 84/sbossert;
92/Slongy; 104–105/levers2007; 106/weintel; 118/vandervelden; 128/Joe
Gough; 140/lisandrotrarbach; 152–3/daniele russo; 154/Sjo; 168/Daisy-
Daisy; 174/Bob Hilscher; 184/The Dan K Experience

Excerpt from '*Buiochas*' le Máirtín Ó Direáin (Máirtín Ó Direáin – *Na
Dánta*) reproduced with kind permission from Cló Iar-Chonnacht.

Every effort has been made to clear permissions for copyrighted material
within the book. In the event of any omissions, the author and publisher
will be glad to rectify this at the earliest opportunity.